Samuel Watson

The Clock Struck One and Christian Spiritualist

Samuel Watson

The Clock Struck One and Christian Spiritualist

ISBN/EAN: 9783337146054

Printed in Europe, USA, Canada, Australia, Japan

Cover: Foto ©Lupo / pixelio.de

More available books at **www.hansebooks.com**

THE CLOCK STRUCK ONE,

AND

CHRISTIAN SPIRITUALIST:

BEING

A SYNOPSIS OF THE INVESTIGATIONS OF SPIRIT INTERCOURSE BY AN EPISCOPAL BISHOP, THREE MINISTERS, FIVE DOCTORS, AND OTHERS, AT MEMPHIS, TENN., IN 1855;

ALSO, THE OPINION OF MANY EMINENT DIVINES, LIVING AND DEAD, ON THE SUBJECT, AND COMMUNICATIONS RECEIVED FROM A NUMBER OF PERSONS RECENTLY.

BY THE

REV. SAMUEL WATSON.

Are they not all ministering spirits, sent forth to minister for them who shall be heirs of salvation?—ST. PAUL.

"TRUTH IS MIGHTY, AND WILL PREVAIL."

LOUISVILLE, KY.:
JOHN P. MORTON AND COMPANY.
1873.

Entered, according to Act of Congress, in the year 1872,

By SAMUEL WATSON,

in the Office of the Librarian of Congress in Washington.

INTRODUCTION.

THE CLOCK STRUCK ONE.

(From the Memphis Appeal.)

"SINGULAR PHENOMENON VOUCHED FOR BY A PROMINENT DIVINE.

"'There are more things in heaven and in earth than are dreamt of in our philosophy.'"

I FIND the following in the last issue of that magnificent paper, the *St. Louis Christian Advocate*. It is not about the extract copied in that paper from the Lexington (Va.) *Gazette*, but the little editorial notice of five lines, to which I wish to call attention:

"A VERY SINGULAR AND MYSTERIOUS OCCURRENCE.

"The Lexington (Va.) *Gazette* publishes the following, asserting that it has received the 'facts' upon undoubted evidence: 'Mr. Z. J. White, whose death occurred last week, was stricken on his return from our last court to his home in Brownsburg, with the disease that proved fatal. On the day of his return he had occasion to go into a room where was kept a clock belonging to his father, the late Robert White. This clock is of the old-fashioned, high kind, and has been stopped for years, not even having the weights attached, being merely kept as a family relic. When Mr. White entered the room, the clock, which had been silent so long, distinctly struck 'one.' He at the time paid no special attention to it, and not being of superstitious turn of mind, thought it was a mistake, or an illusion of his fancy. The next day, or the day after, he again had occasion to enter the same room. Again the clock struck 'one.' He immediately went out, telling his wife of the circumstance, and remarked that he felt assured he was going to die soon. His premonitions, as we have stated, proved true, and in a few days his spirit passed away.

"There is nothing singular nor mysterious in it. Such results of panic in persons of superstitious imagination are familiar to all who have paid any attention to the morbid relations of mind and brain."

I will give some facts which have come under my own observation and that of others, which no doubt will, in the estimation of the author of those lines, place me, and others in the category of persons of "superstitious imagination." It is popular with some people to ridicule facts when they have no evidence of disproving them, or argument to overthrow them. It is the easiest way to dispose of many things that occur which can not be accounted for upon any hypothesis or theory with which they are familiar.

Five years since I was at my place with my family, in Woodruff county, near Augusta, Arkansas. My wife's health had been feeble for a long time. Her physician had told me, before we went over there, that she might die in twenty-four hours. Her health was partially restored after a few months residence there. She was, however, taken with her old disease, and after a few days' illness she died. On the mantel in her room was an old clock which had not run or struck for years, only once, which was the day before she died. A little over a year afterward, a noble boy of about four years, named after Robert E. Lee, was taken sick, lived a few days, the clock struck one, and the next day he died.

The following summer my daughters visited my brother, Dr. K. P. Watson, near Memphis, and took with them their youngest brother, Durell. He had always been a very healthy child, but was taken sick at my brother's, and in few hours died. The clock on the mantel in Arkansas struck once again, and in a few hours we received a dispatch that Durell was dead.

The next autumn the clock struck again, and our Lillian, a babe of six months of age, passed away from us to join those who had gone before.

One more case. My father died in that neighborhood about twelve years since. Brother Coleman, the preacher on the Augusta circuit, lived that year on the place. There was about such a clock as is described by the *Gazette*. "It is of the old-fashioned, high kind, and has been stopped for years, not even having the weights attached," but was packed away up stairs with some lumber ever since the death of my father. Brother Coleman's child was sick, the clock struck "one," the child died soon after.

I have given you the facts, Mr. Editor, even at the risk of being called superstitious. I need not give you my explanation or theory, but I would like to have yours. All of these times, were in the daytime that the clock struck, and it was heard by different members of the family every time.

Were you not in Dr. A. H. Redford's office, when we were together in Nashville recently, when he told us of the glass breaking over

INTRODUCTION.   v

the picture of Bishop Andrew? You remember he has a fine likeness of all the Bishops hanging against the wall in his office. It seems—it may be superstitious to believe it, but Dr. Redford told it to quite a number of preachers—that about the time the Bishop was attacked with what produced his death, the glass broke over his picture. I then told them what I have written of the clock striking, etc.

Yesterday evening, as I was going home, I met a friend at the door of a music store on Main Street. A gentleman came in just then with his arms full of picture-frames. I mentioned the fact of the glass of Bishop Andrew's picture breaking. He said he had known of a number of similar cases. There are many things occurring equally "singular and mysterious," but people do not like to be called "superstitious," and hence rarely mention them, for fear of it. I ask the question, are these "results of panic," or "the morbid relations of mind and brain?" as you said of the Virginia case. Or are they given us to demonstrate one of the most consoling doctrines taught in the Bible? I leave my friends of the *St. Louis Christian Advocate*, or any one else, to answer to the satisfaction of many anxious inquirers after truth, was it "panic" that caused the clock to strike when the child was over a hundred miles distant, and we had not the slightest knowledge of his having been sick.

SAMUEL WATSON.

I propose to give Dr. Bond's editorials and my reply to them, that the public may see this matter from the beginning. He introduced some things which I considered irrelevant to the subject under consideration. I have therefore omited them and my reply to them, because they have no bearing on the subject under discussion.

(From the St. Louis Christian Advocate.)
"THE CLOCK STRUCK ONE."

"'The root of all superstition is, that to the nature of the mind of all men it is consonant for the affirmative or active to effect more than the negative or privative; so that a few times hitting or presence countervails oftimes failing or absence.'—BACON: *Adv. of Learning*.

"In our paper of June 12th we read, at our home in Maryland, a letter from Rev. Samuel Watson, occasioned by a few remarks we had appended to a story about the supernatural relations of the bell of an old clock to a divination of death. As we understand Christianity to require us to defend society, as much as we can, against the powerful, natural tendency to magic, which from the days of Moses we have authority to recognize as the most vivacious of the enemies of the truth, we wrote a few lines to deny the inference of the supernatural in the matter. Bro. Watson comes valiantly to the defence of the miraculous in the clock, and in the full assurance of his faith in its premonitions, rebukes us as belonging to a class 'who ridicule facts when they have no evidence disproving them, or arguments to overpower them.' We certainly manifested no such disposition. We did not *ridicule the facts*, nor even deny them. We admitted that the old clock struck, and that the man who heard it subsequently died. These were the only *facts* in the statement. What we *denied* was, the unjustifiable inference that the clock struck because the man was about to die, and *struck* by miraculous interposition of the power and prescience of God. If it did, that old clock is as awful as the burning bush in which God appeared to Moses. It is an oracle of death, more terrible than the Ark of God, which did *not* foretell the death of men. We denied the miracle, and suggested a rational explanation. Bro. Watson, no doubt, thinks that explanation improbable. Suppose it is, at least it is *possible*, and *any possible explanation of a physical phenomenon is more probable—in other words, more entitled to belief—than a miracle; for it is the very essence of a miracle that it is absolutely improbable in nature.* We would not be justified in believing any miracle recorded in Scripture if we could account for the facts stated upon natural principles. The overwhelming force of the miracles that attested our religion, is secured to us only by insisting upon this inexorable canon of criticism.

"We are sincerely anxious to avoid giving offense to Bro. Watson. He is very sensitive to the charge of being superstitious. He need not be so sensitive. He has the great majority of people with him—perhaps there are a few who could show themselves clear of superstition upon close examination. The term is offensive, but the condition is almost universal. The greater part of the Christian world are but little freer from it than the worshipers of the *first* deities whose busts filled the Pantheon.

"Among the most educated, the blood is yet infected with the virus of the old magic. Dr. Johnson went through the streets touching posts, and was careful to put the safe foot foremost in leaving a house. The late Emperor and Empress of France consulted witches and mediums. Queen Victoria, and her ladies, followed her just-married daughter to her carriage, and sent good luck after her in a shower of old shoes. We think few ladies would be married on Friday. Countless omens and magical formulas are in activity every day in the houses of Protestants, who seem utterly unconscious of the sin and shame of fearing other gods than their Father in heaven.

"We would not reply to Bro. Watson if we could conscientiously avoid it; but the challenge he has thrown out is too serious to be passed over. To admit the supernaturalism of the clock, would be to do mischief far beyond the sound of discarded and dilapidated time-keepers. It would be to admit and uncontrollable irruption of the old magism into the church. It would be to give the sanction of religion to the undefined, distressing, and degrading superstition, that is one of the most remarkable characteristics of the carnal mind. If clocks, occasionally, become moved with knowledge of impending death, how are we to deny to the trembling rustic *his* privilege of omen in the howling of his dog, or the cry of the whip-po-will? How are we to laugh away the terror of sounds in a bedstead, or cracks in a looking-glass? All these ominous voices will be accredited to us by *facts;* and upon what principle shall we contradict them? For instance, it is what we dare to call a superstition, that it is a prevision of death for thirteen to sit at a table. We know respectable, well-educated people who would go without dinner rather than be the thirteenth. Bro. Watson will probably laugh at this nonsense. Yet, not long ago, at the table of a wealthy merchant in Baltimore, a lady happened to take her seat as the thirteenth. It was observed, and she was warned; yet she persisted. Before the end of the year she died. Now, how, if we admit the possibility of truth in such things, are we to discriminate between clocks and other oracles? Evidently there would be no definite line between faith and superstition, and the two would soon become confused into one. We do not mean, however, that the serious consequences of admitting Bro. Watson's claims for his oracular clock should prevent us from giving full force to his facts; but only that they should compel us to make a proper inquiry into his statements

"Without going any further, too, we are able, on the other hand, to assure Bro. Watson, that Bishop Andrew's picture is not the only one in which the glass sympathized with the original. Just before the battle of Gettysburg, a picture of Mr. Davis suddenly fell and hid its face behind a bed, and broke its glass. It is *a fact*, which we hold ourselves responsible for, *extraordinary as it is*. We do not, however, believe that God wrought a miracle to break the glass in Mr. Davis' portrait, or Bishop Andrew's either. We do not consider miracle as the most natural, easy, and lawful of all explanations of obscure phenomena. We have no faith in the mortuary relations of glass, nor the dismal forebodings of clock-hammers. Many strange things are very easily understood, when once the key is found. Mystery in nature is only ignorance of nature.

"In the last century it was gravely stated, in a history of the Island of St. Kilda, that the arrival of a stranger gave the people cold. The author, Rev. Dr. Macauley, was very averse to superstitions, but he had to admit the fact. Dr. John Campbell took a great deal of pains to ascertain the truth, and found it established, beyond doubt. He did not, however, solve the problem by the ready application of a "miracle;" but he tried to explain the fact by some theory of human effluvia. He was wrong. The fact was not explained; still, there was no necessity for calling in miracle to explain it. The cause was only unknown. All that was known was the relation between the arrival of strangers and prevalent colds. Afterward, a few words explained the mystery. An 'ingenious gentleman,' in other words, a man of mind fitted for such inquiries (Mr. Dorking,) as soon as the problem was stated, saw the secret, which was only a disregarded but patent fact. Strangers could only arrive at the island *with a north-east wind*. The clock mystery will be solved in the same way. In the meantime, let us be satisfied with the '*living oracles*,' and place no confidence in old clocks and cracked glass. We have no reason to believe that God speaks to us in such ways.

"We have no reason to believe that he can communicate better with people who have old clocks than with others; or that picture-frames partake of the powers of the lost Urim and Thummim. This may be called *ridicule ;* but it is the expression of serious common sense. Skepticism, of all marvelous assumptions, is the state of mind proper for the investigation of a truth.

"As we began with one quotation from Bacon, we will conclude with another:

"'Another error is, impatience of doubt, and haste to assertion, without due and mature suspension of judgment. *If a man will begin with certainties, he shall end in doubt ; but if he will be content to begin with doubt, he shall end in certainties.*'

"Our answer to Bro. Watson's peremptory challenge is, that we do not believe that his clock strikes only just before the death of one of his family. All that we believe is, that in several instances the clock has been *noticed* to strike precedent to such deaths. In three of the instances the observers were watching by the side of the dying, and the striking could not pass unobserved. We believe it struck when it was not noticed, for such is a natural and reasonable conclusion, and *there is no evidence to disprove it*. Apart from the 'superstition' about its connection with death, if Bro. Watson should have told us that he heard the clock strike on the four several occasions, but that it never struck except on these four, nobody would have admitted his statement. Everybody would have believed it more likely that it struck when it was not noticed, than that it was noticed every time it struck. Particularly is this opinion reasonable, when, if we admit that the striking was always noticed, we must admit, too, the astounding coincidences."

Thus endeth Dr. Bond's broadside at the "old clock, superstition," etc.

The following is my reply to it:

Rev. Dr. Bond—*Dear Sir:* On my return from Arkansas I found your editorial notice of my article respecting the striking of an old clock. I thank you for the respectful consideration you have given it. It was to call forth your opinion that I wrote the notice I did of your editorial respecting the article copied from the *Lexington* (Virginia) *Gazette*. Having read your paper with much interest from its commencement, and your father's (the old *Advocate and Journal* of New York) from its beginning, in my boyhood, I have always entertained for him a respect amounting to almost veneration, a portion of which has descended to his son.

I said "I have given you the facts Mr. Editor, at the risk of being called superstitious. I need not give you my explanation or theory, but would like to have yours." I infer from your reply that you suppose my theory to be that whenever an old clock strikes, some member of the family dies. I did not design to convey such an idea, for I had never heard of such a coincidence before, but have heard of several since, as well-authenticated as human testimony can make them. You erect that man of straw and concentrate your batteries in nearly three columns of your mammoth sheet to demolish him. The leading thought in this well-matured article—as may be gathered from what you say influenced you in noticing the article from the *Gazette*—is "to defend society as much as we can against the powerful tendency to magic." I would ask the Doctor if the Scriptures do not teach, under every dispensation, that there have been angelic ministrations to mankind? Does not Mr. Wesley, Dr. Clarke, Richard Watson and all the standard authorities of Methodism teach the same doctrine?

Mr. Wesley quotes the language of Socrates, where he says "My demon did not give me notice this morning of any evil that was to befall me to-day; therefore I cannot regard as any evil my being condemned to die." Mr. Wesley says "undoubtedly it was some spiritual being, probably one of these ministering ghosts."

Dr. Clarke, our most learned commentator, says:

"1. I believe there is a supernatural and spiritual world in which human spirits, both good and bad, live in a state of conciousness.

"2. I believe there is an invisible world, in which various orders of spirits, not human, live and act.

"3. I believe that any of these spirits may, according to the order of God in the laws of their place of residence, have intercourse with this world, and become visible to mortals."

I could quote from others to the same effect to show that this is, and always has been held by the founders and the highest authority known to the Methodist Church. You say "Brother Watson comes valiantly to the defense of the miraculous in the clock." You misunderstand me, for I have never considered the striking of a clock miraculous. Mr. Watson, in his Biblical Dictionary, gives from Dr. Samuel Clarke the definition of a miracle: "A miracle is a work effected in a manner unusual or different from the common and regular method of providence, by the interposition of God himself, or some intelligent agent superior to man, for the proof or evidence of some particular doctrine, or in attestation of the authority of some particular person." I do not believe there was any agency "superior to man," in his spiritual state, engaged in this matter of the clock striking—matter is certainly no obstruction to a ministering spirit giving the result of the disease that is preying upon the vitals of the physical system so that death must necessarily soon be accomplished.

The moving of an old clock-hammer would be as easily done as many other things they do, and would be as likely to arrest attention as anything, especially when it was impossible for anything to get in the clock of a physical nature. The striking of our clock was invariably in the day-time and heard by all the members of the family who were present. I brought this clock over to have it repaired. It is now in the office of the *Western Methodist*, where any one can see that no cat, rat, mouse or even fly, could get into it. Enough on the clock question—assuring you, Doctor, that there is nothing "awful" about it—nothing like the burning bush in which God appeared to Moses. It was simply one of the thousand ways that those who minister to us manifest their presence and the interest they feel in our welfare. There is nothing about it of a miraculous character, as I understand it. You say: "He [I] has the great majority of the people with him. Perhaps there are few who could show themselves clear of superstition upon close examination. The term is offensive, but the condition is almost universal. The greater part of the Christian world are but little freer from it than the worshipers of the first deities whose busts filled the pantheon." Superstition, as defined by Webster, is a belief in the direct agency of superior powers in certain extraordinary or irregular events, or in omens and prognostics. Would you not class our Saviour with "the majority of mankind" in this respect? Did not he have communication with, not only angelic, but with departed human beings, while he tabernacled among men? Did not he believe and teach the "direct agency of superior power?" I have no doubt that he would be classed among the superstitous by some who claim to be above "the morbid state of mind and brain" of the majority of mankind. I have found many who would ridicule things of this character, and yet, before the communication closed, they would tell of things more mysterious than that at which they had sneered. Again you say "Countless omens and magical formulas are in activity every day in the house; Protestants, who seem utterly unconscious of the sin and shame of fearing other gods than their Father in heaven———." I have been taught to believe, upon the authority of the Bible, that our "Heavenly Father" gave his angels charge over us, "the angel of the Lord encampeth around those that fear him and delivereth them," and that they are "all ministering spirits, sent forth to minister to those who should be heirs of salvation." There is "no fearing of other gods" in all this. Nothing of which any one should be "ashamed;" but one of the most consolatory doctrines taught in the Bible.

You say: "We would not reply to Brother Watson if we could conscientiously avoid it, but the challenge he throws out is too serious to be passed over." Well, Doctor, I have accomplished the object I had in view by writing what I did. I knew you were in the habit of giving such things a lick, whenever you had an opportunity of doing so. I knew also you were capable of representing the other side of that question as well, or better, than any one of my acquaintances; not only from your capacity, but from your profession of M. D., idiosyncrasy, etc., etc. Hence I said "I need not give you my explanation or theory, but would like to have yours." You have given some kinds of superstition of which

I never heard; and your prediction that "Brother Watson will probably laugh at this nonsense" has been literally fulfilled.

You give one illustration, however, Doctor, that is of too serious a character to even smile at—what you say in your last paragraph about Mr. Davis' picture:

I consider this a very significant fact. The battle of Gettysburg was the crisis in the history of the Southern Confederacy. Had General Lee been successful there we have been assured that the Confederacy would have been acknowledged by England and France; as they had promised to do if the issue of that battle had been favorable to the Confederates.

Mr. Davis was the head of the Confederacy, and a representative man. The breaking of the glass over his picture, its suddenly falling, and its hiding its face behind a bed, were certainly "astounding concidences;" much more so than the striking of an old clock, just before a member of my family died. Tis true Mr. Davis did not die, for I saw him coming out of his church door as I passed from church on Sabbath last; but the Southern Confederacy set in death on that field of blood, and thousands of soldiers sealed their devotion to the "lost cause;" with as good blood as was ever shed on a battle-field. I admit the truth of the last sentence quoted from you, that "mystery of nature is only ignorance of nature," but sir, this is beyond nature or natural law, so far as I have been able to learn. It belongs to another state of things. The natural man comprehendeth not the spiritual things. They are spiritually discerned. The "many things are very easily understood when once the key is found." That is also true, but where is the key? I think that it will be found that it is only that kind of a key which unlocked Peter's prison door that will ever unlock the things of which we are writing. Neither your physical science nor medical jurisprudence understand it, but rather shows its ignorance of such things by attempting it. I am "sincerely anxious to avoid giving offense" to you, Doctor, for I think you have been "sincerely desirous to discharge a duty you believe you owe the readers of your paper and the church." You have done as well, perhaps, as any one could with your view of the subject. I assure you that you have not given me the slightest offense. I have been delighted with your manly, Christian reply to my article. You have treated me as a Christian brother, and given the subject, as I think it deserves, a calm investigation.

If you are disposed to publish this, and reply to it, I should be pleased to have the privilege of discussing these matters from a

Bible stand-point with you. I wish to say nothing more about our old clock, let it go to its regular business, for I think it has accomplished its mission; but let us discuss these questions as Christian ministers wishing to ascertain the truth.

With sentiments of the highest regard for you personally and officially, I am yours, truly, SAMUEL WATSON.

(Editorial from Advocate.)

"THE MYSTERY OF THE CLOCK.

"We find, in a slip sent us from the *Memphis Avalanche*, the reply of Rev. Samuel Watson to some remarks we made upon the supposed connection between the irregular striking of his clock and the succeeding death of several of his family. Accompanying the slip was a kindly letter from Bro. Watson, expressing a wish that we should reprint his reply and continue the discussion of the subject. (His reply appeared in our issue of last week.) Considering it to be a very important thing to reach some definite understanding with regard to the discriminations of faith, concerning which there is, even in deeply pious minds, a great deal of confusion and error, we cheerfully accede to the request. There is credulity, there is superstition, there is reasonable faith in the miraculous and the supernatural. Credulity and superstition are enemies to all truth, and among the strongest of the opponents to the Gospel. Faith is the evidence, the assurance, the practical realization of truth, particularly of the fundamental truths of religion. That it can be distinguished from its enemies is certain; but they have donned its uniform, and imitated its speech, and stolen into its camp, and they cannot be detected by a superficial observation.

"It would have been a very great convenience if Bro. Watson had told us distinctly what he does believe about that clock. It would have saved him and us a good deal of trouble if we had known that he believes as we do, that old clocks, not in use, do occasionally strike, without the unexpected sound being followed by the entrance of the Pale Horse. If Bro. Watson had noticed the striking and the contemporaneous deaths only as curious coincidences we would not have troubled him with our criticism. The coincidences concerned us only when the two incidents were presented as related in dependence, and procured by supernatural agency for the purpose of conveying preternatural intelligence. If Bro. Watson did not mean that, there is nothing for us to discuss. Bro. Watson says there was nothing "miraculous" in the affair. So we think. But though not 'miraculous,' he thinks it supernatural. We confess we do not understand the distinction. The striking was natural, or contrary to the operation of natural laws. The rule of nature was for the clock to be quiet. Bro. Watson thinks that a spirit, independent of the laws of matter, possessed of information beyond the power of human faculties, commissioned by God to minister to a certain person, or persons, did, for moral purposes of God, overcome the natural condition of the clock and cause it to strike. If this is not miracle none is recorded. Bro. Watson quotes from 'Watson's Dictionary,' 'A miracle is a work effected in a manner unusual or different from the common and regular methods of Providence, by the interposition of God himself or some intelligent agent superior to man, for the proof or evidence of some particular doctrine, or in attestation of the authority of some particular person.' He then declares, 'I do not believe there was any agency superior to man in his spiritual state engaged in this matter of the clock. What agency was it, then? No man could know that a death had taken place at the distance in question. No man could put his finger through the case of the clock, without mechanical injury to it, and touch the hammer, without violating the law that two bodies can not occupy the same space at the same time. No man could be invisible before the eyes of other men. We think the agent, if there was one, was very superior to man in intelligence and powers of *penetration* into disease and through the clock. But suppose he was inferior, would the strange work be less miraculous? When Balaam's ass spake he was "inferior to man." The raven that brought Elijah his food was "inferior to man." Were they not miracles that these messengers of God accomplished?'

"But it is useless to quibble about words, for Bro. Watson goes on to show plainly his theory of the affair. 'Matter is certainly no obstruction to a ministering spirit giving the result of the disease that is preying upon the vitals of the physical system so that death must soon be necessarily accomplished.' So it was a 'ministering spirit' that struck the clock—a spirit not 'superior to man in his spiritual state'—a spirit immaterial and unaffected by matter. We have heard too much of this language not to understand that Bro. Watson believes the agent to have been the spirit of a dead human being. He has adopted the spiritist assumption, that disembodied spirits are 'superior to man' in knowledge; and that while they can, in a small way, act upon matter, they are not obstructed by it. Bro. Watson accepts the doctrine, that mankind are subject to the operations of spirits, whose communications are not messages from

God, but only the tender of their superior information. Matter being 'no obstruction' to them, they see the progress of disease to a fatal issue, and wood or brass being no obstruction, they make a clock strike to give information of what is coming. Now, in all this, there are several tremendous assumptions, of infinite importance in their consequences, and *we deny every one of them.* It is now for Bro. Watson to prove, or at least to show us, some reasonable probability for believing,

"1. That the spirits of the dead have superior information about human affairs, and superior facility in communicating it to persons at a distance. That they have such a knowledge of pathology as to know when diseases are to be fatal.

"2. That matter is no obstruction to these spirits. Bro. Watson says it 'certainly' is not. Upon what grounds is this 'certainty' built? For ourselves, we confess that we have no knowledge whatever, natural or revealed, that teaches us any such thing.

"3. They do 'a thousand things.' or any number of things, as hard as handling the hammer of the old clock, without regard to the 'obstruction' of its case. We deny it. We know no evidence of it. The Bible gives none. Experience gives none. Bro. Watson must give us proof. He says a fly could not get into the clock, but he wants us to believe a ghost did. We can not do it. We know flies, but we do not know ghosts. We do not know that there are any in the world. We think there are not. We consider them very badly fitted to live in it. It is a material world. Bodyless human beings are of no use here, and there is no provision for their comfort. If matter does not obstruct them, they can do nothing with matter. But we should like to know how a touch could press a spring, if matter did not 'obstruct' or resist the finger. We use matter because it resists us. A bird flies, a ship sails, a man walks, because of the resistance of matter. There is no revelation nor reason to sustain such an assumption as the presence and agency of human ghosts acting upon the world outside of the laws of matter. With regard to the motor power of the old clock, if 'no rat, cat, nor fly moved it,' then we suppose it was shaken by a step on some part of the floor, which had peculiar mechanical relations to the spot where the clock stood. If that be not the explanation, we will put the clock story in our heap of things yet to be explained, and let it bide its time. We do not feel justified to raise the dead, and invest them with unintelligible superior-inferiority and material-immateriality only to strike a clock-hammer.

"Is Bro. Watson serious in his grave treatment of the fall of Mr. Davis' picture? Does he really think that some spirit, full of the news of carnal warfare, hurried to Baltimore to announce it to a few ladies, and, after all, could devise no better way to tell it than to go into the garret, and take down a cheap picture, and put it behind the bed, where it was not found until the result of the battle was told in the newspapers? If Bro. Watson really 'considers this a very significant fact,' we do not wonder that he hears and sees marvelous things; for he certainly has a remarkable aptitude for seeing 'significance' where others see nothing remarkable at all. We have no difficulty in accounting for the fall of the photograph. Hundreds probably fall every day. It was not a valuable work of art. It was not secured with particular care. If the nail did not enter a crevice between the bricks, or if it took defective hold of the mortar, the pressure would loosen it after a while, and it is quite possible that the thunder of several hundred heavy cannon, even as far off as Gettysburg, might so agitate the earth, as to cause a tremor in the fourth story of a house, whose walls are not at all thick, sufficient to shake down a loose picture. Sometimes a picture falls because a string wears and breaks. Indeed, we humbly think that the law of gravitation is quite equal to the fall of that photograph, without help from Puck or any imaginary spirit. The reason why the picture hid behind the bed, is not difficult to find. The bed was before it, and even 'the natural man' can comprehend why the picture should, therefore, be behind.

"Bro. Watson asks us several questions that we do not think at all pertinent. He asks whether the Scriptures do not teach the ministration of angels? Certainly. What then? Bro. Watson is contending for a class of ministering spirits 'not superior to man in his spiritual state.' He disowns the connection of God or angels with the clock. We are not discussing the general question of ministering angels, but the special question, whether 'ministering spirits,' not angels, touched the old clock. Let us keep to the point, or we can settle nothing. Bro. Watson asks if we do not include our Lord among the superstitious of mankind? Certainly not. We have never said that a belief 'in superior power,' nor in the agency of angels, was superstitious; nor intimated that it was unreasonable for the Incarnate God to communicate with the angels or spirits. Jesus called back the dead. We should think it grossly superstitious for Bro. Watson to presume that *he* could do it. Again, all that Bro. Watson says about angelic administrations is gratuitous and out of place. We must attend to our own affair. We must confine ourselves to our own spirits. If Bro. Watson will give up his familiar ghosts, and say that an angel touched his clock, we will discuss that; but as long as he rejects angelic agency in the matter, we will, with his permission, let the angels alone. With regard to Mr Wesley's opinion about Socrates' demon, we have only to say, that on that subject Mr. Wesley knew no more than the rest of us. We have no hesitation in saying that we do not believe that Socrates had any ministering angel to give him notice of coming evil. He had as much evil as other men. He was subjected to all the inconveniences of opposing popular opinions, and, besides, he suffered grievous things from the tongue and hands of his wife, Xantippe. At last he was poisoned, and died professing his faith in the gods, and asking that a cock should be sacrificed to an idol on his behalf. Neither Mr. Wesley, nor anybody else, has adduced any evidence of the supernaturalism of the Socrates demon. We do not think that Socrates believed it himself, or intended others to believe it. It is a long way to go for evidence about the old clock, and the journey is unprofitable.

"But Bro. Watson is done with the supernaturalism of the clock. He will have it mended and set to its lawful uses. If his opinions be true, it is a pity; for he is cutting off one of the recognized channels of intercourse with spirits, who, of all created intelligences, seem to have the greatest difficulty in making themselves understood. Dumb men make signs that are readily comprehended. The ignorant keeper of an ale-house can keep a score on his door with chalk; but the spirits knock with wretched, abortive telegraphy upon tables, or crack their tokens with the borrowed tendons of a lying leg, or gibber their senseless message in the incoherent, grammarless thief-language of a mercenary medium, or, according to Bro. Watson, after having gone a long distance with a message of death, can find no way to tell it but by making a clock strike a wrong hour; which, in fact, is telling nothing at all. Poor, dumb ministering spirit this is! We would rather be ministered to by the postman or telegraph boy. Yet, as Bro. Watson's clock was one of the few things spirits could play on, 'tis a pity to remove its inward uncleanness, and restore order to its machinery. For it is a curious thing that the spirits are neither visible nor audible, except when something is out of order. To be sure, Bro. Watson says the clock was only 'one of a thousand ways' in which the spirits manifest their presence. Will he be so good as to name to us some of the remaining nine hundred and ninety-nine? We know none of them. We have heard of innumerable signs and omens. Bro. Watson laughed at one we told him of, but we know of none more reliable. Which of the signs is true? We particularly desire Bro. Watson to tell us. Of a thousand, we ought to know some.

> "'Matrons who toss the cup, and see
> The grounds of fate in grounds of tea'

have long tradition on their side, and are fortified, no doubt, with ample coincidences. Do the spirits arrange "the grounds of fate?" Does not Bro. Watson see the danger of such vague and positive statements with regard to a matter of such transcendent importance? Does he not see the necessity we are under of pressing him to tell us upon what grounds he believes in this facile communication with the spiritual world, and which of the 'thousand ways' he advises the readers of his articles to trust in as oracles of fate or warnings of God, or, at least, as evidence 'of the presence of ministering spirits.'

"We have no objection at all to discuss all the questions Bro. Watson suggests. But we wait now for his reply to our request for the evidence upon which his statements about spirits are based."

REPLY TO "THE MYSTERY OF THE CLOCK."

DEAR DR. BOND: I find an editorial of two and a half columns in your paper of the 9th, in reply to what I said respecting the striking of an old clock. I fully agree with you as to the importance of discriminating between credulity, superstition, and faith. "Credulity," Webster says, is "a disposition to believe on slight evidence, or no evidence at all." Superstition has general significations, but that to which you refer I suppose is "the belief of what is absurd, or belief without evidence," "or a belief in the direct agency of superior powers in certain extraordinary or singular events." Faith is the assent of the mind to the truth of a proposition advanced by another—belief on probable evidence of any kind. Faith depends upon evidence—testimony; and according to the character of the testimony will be the strength of our faith. We must not, we can not, ignore human testimony. All the faith we possess depends upon that, except our own experience and consciousness of what we have received through our senses. The foundation of our holy Christianity rests, to a very great extent, upon human testimony.

In reply to your inquiry as to what I think of that clock, I will simply state that at first I attached no importance to it. But when it struck four times only (all that was ever heard), and at each of those times a member of my family died, I was compelled to believe there was something more than "curious coincidences" connected therewith. That there was premonition of an afflictive event is certain; but as to the cause of its thus striking, and the power by which it was done, is the question about which we differ. Let us leave that old clock to do its original work. I am receiving, by letter and verbally, almost every day, as "astonishing coincidences" as its striking under the circumstances. They do not come from the "credulous, superstitious" part of mankind, but from men and women of the very best minds and hearts in the land, embracing ministers of the different churches, physicians of the highest standing, and editors whose testimony could not be questioned. I select from a prominent minister of the M. E. Church, South. He is the father of one of the pastors of the church in this city.

"FULTON STATION, Ky., *July* 17, 1871.
"OTHER OLD CLOCKS.

"A child died in a family residing in Benton county, Arkansas. An old clock belonging to the family, which had not been in use for many years, struck one the day before the child died. Several years subsequently the father of the child died, and the old clock, which had not struck since the death of the child, struck one, and no more. In Evansville, Illinois, an old clock, which had long been silent, struck one the day before the death of a member of the family owning the clock. Subsequently another member of the family died, and the same old clock struck one and ceased.

"S. G. PATTERSON,
"Father of Rev. Wm. Patterson, of the Memphis Conference."

One more old clock and I pass on. During the war, a Confederate general was at the house of Mr. B., in Aberdeen, Miss. There was quite a number of friends discussing the question of persons returning after death and making themselves known. There was in the room an old clock which had not run or struck for many years. The general told them if he got killed, or died during the war, that if he could, he would come back and make that old clock strike. It was agreed upon, and so understood by all the party. The Confederate general was killed, and soon after the clock struck, while some of the party were in the room, which so alarmed them that they fled in haste out of the room, if not out of the house. I give this upon the highest authority in the Methoist Episcopal Church, South.

Now, Doctor, if you feel disposed, turn your batteries on some other old clocks besides mine. Their theory and mine is the same.

You seem solicitous for my theory, and desirous for me to give to you some of the "many ways spirits minister to us." Well, Doctor, I will be happy to gratify you in this respect. I believe with St. Paul, that there is an "outward man" and an "inward man." The former of the "earth, earthy," the other the intellectual, moral, spiritual man, that is not subject to death. I agree with Dr. Adam Clarke, the most learned commentator that ever wrote, when he says: "I believe there is a supernatural and spiritual world in which human spirits live, and have intercourse with this world, and become visible to mortals." I believe that this "spiritual world" is to spiritual beings as *real* and as *tangible* as the *physical world* is to our *natural bodies;* that this spiritual world surrounds the natural world, and, for aught I know, may extend throughout the immensity of space; that this is the paradise or place of departed spirits, in that intermediate state between death and the resurrection. I agree with Bishop Morris, the senior Bishop of the M. E. Church, when he says: "There is a clear distinction made in the Sacred Scriptures between the intermediate and final state after the general resurrection;" also with one of our Bishops when he says: "No one has yet been saved in heaven; no one sent to hell. These states and conditions will not be awarded till the judgment, and it will not take place till the resurrection." And with another one of our Bishops, who says: "We labor not only in the sight of mortals, we labor also in the sight of celestial beings. We preach to two congregations at the same moment, one below and the other above us."

Man's *intellectual, moral* or *spiritual*, is a refined substance, a "spiritual body," which constitutes his individuality—his personality. The real man never dies. The "outward man" does; but the "inner man" passes through the veil which divides the natural from the spiritual world, identically the same being he was here. What we call death does not change the *moral status* of our spiritual nature. He now has employment suitable to his spiritual surroundings and desires. I believe that every Christian has one or more of these "guardian angels," or "ministering spirits," as St. Paul calls them, who watch over us. The affection they had for loved ones is not broken by death; they still love us and feel a deep interest in all that pertains to our welfare, and do all they can, consistently with our moral agency, to lead us in the paths of virtue, and, ultimately, to the better land. Then we, with the same attractions to loved ones left behind, engage in the same glorious work, and thus develop our capacity to enjoy, by consecrating it all to the promotion of the interests of the Redeemer's kingdom.——But I am wandering.

You say: "It is now for Bro. Watson to prove, or, at least, to give us some reasonable probability for believing: 1st, That the spirits of the dead have superior information about human affairs, and superior faculty in communicating it to persons at a distance." They would certainly be poorly qualified to minister to us if they did not possess those requisites. Mortal vision is, at best, imperfect. St. Paul says, 1 Cor. xiii. 12: "For now we see through a glass, darkly; but then face to face: now I know in part; but then shall I know even as also I am known." I think the apostle has answered that question satisfactorily to most minds.

2. "That matter is no obstruction to these spirits. . . . For ourselves, we confess that we have no knowledge whatever, natural or revealed, that teaches us any such thing."

Does Dr. Bond suppose that the thousands who have died surrounded by walls of granite and iron, that they (the walls) were any obstruction to the soul's liberty, after the death of the body? I will not insult his good sense by even insinuating that he does.

3. "That they do any number of things as hard as handling the hammer of an old clock. We deny it. We know no evidence of it. The Bible gives none. Experience gives none. Bro. Watson must give us proof."

To answer the above, I shall be compelled to mention some things that will subject me to the charge of "credulity, superstition," etc. So be it. I am willing to bear it, for—

"Truth, crushed to earth, will rise again;
The eternal years of God are her's."

My maxim is:

"To seize the truth wherever found,
On Christian or on heathen ground."

I do not propose, however, to go only on "Christian ground" for the purpose of "giving proof" of what I have seen and heard on this subject. I have been the pastor of the different Methodist churches in this city since 1839. In the course of my pastoral visits I have met with a considerable number of persons in the proper exercise of their mental faculties, who have assured me that for weeks before their dissolution, they saw, recognized, and conversed with their friends, who were in the spiritual world. One of these still lingers upon a bed of affliction. They accord with what Dr. Clarke says: "These spirits have intercourse with this world, and become visible to mortals." I select one individual be cause of his high position as the head of the Protestant Episcopal Church in Tennessee. Bishop Otey, years before he died, told me that he had always believed in the doctrine of "ministering spirits," but that he now knew they were around him; that he conversed with them, etc., etc. His daughter, who had passed away years before, performed on the guitar, or he told me she did, when no one was present in the room but himself; also, upon the harp, playing the favorite tunes she played for him while living. Bro. Tippet, long a member of the North Carolina Conference, was sick a long time in this city. I visited him frequently. He used to tell me that his spirit friends came to see him daily. He saw them, not with the natural, but with the spiritual eye.

There are a number of gentlemen and ladies in this city now who have told me that they see and converse with their relatives daily. They are not what are called Spiritualists, but they are influential members of the different churches, with as clear heads and as good hearts as others. Not long since, as I was passing along our main thoroughfare to Sabbath school, I stopped to speak with two gentlemen friends. One was telling the other he had a brother who had been dead for four years; that he saw and conversed with him often, and that he was more company for him than any other of his relatives. Others have said the same.

I think it likely that the "man's hand" that wrote Belshazzar's doom on the wall, was a fit subject for ridicule by the incredulous of that day. Don't you think, Doctor, that "the man who appeared to Manoah's wife" so frequently, or the "man of Macedonia" who "prayed him [St. Paul], saying, Come over to Macedonia and help us," could have made an old clock strike one?

Once more. You say: "If Bro. Watson will give up his familiar ghosts, and say that an angel touched his clock, we will discuss that; but as long as he rejects angelic agency in the matter, we will, with his permission, let the angels alone."

I use the term angel as the Scriptures do, as synonymous with man. The term simply means messenger, and is applied to man under every dispensation in the Scriptures. We have not now time to discuss this question. I still maintain that there is nothing miraculous (your opinion to the contrary notwithstanding) in any of the things I have mentioned. They are in perfect accord with the laws of the spiritual world in which they live; and it is part of their employment and enjoyment thus to "to minister to those who shall be heirs of salvation."

One word more. You say, "The spirits knock with wretched

telegraphy on tables." Now, Doctor, if you have any design to refer to "modern spiritualism," as it is understood, I respectfully decline any further reply to anything you may say. I never go to such places, have nothing to do with such things, and have not the slightest reference to them in what I have said; nor do I know that any of the parties I have mentioned do. Our discussion must be, as I said before, from a Bible stand-point, the standard authorities of the church, and the testimony of reliable witnesses.

SAMUEL WATSON.

(Editorial from Advocate.)

THE OLD CLOCK.

"The reply to us, by Bro. Watson in the *Advocate* of August 31, reveals a painful if not surprising prevalence in the Church, and among enlightened men, of the opinions which underlie the gross and atheistic *spiritism* that is working such frightful moral desolation in the community. It is easy now to comprehend how the wretched jugglery of the Fox girls, and the wild ravings of incoherent mediums, have found favor and gathered discipleship, and how Christian faith has been abandoned for a superstition as groveling as confidence in an African fetisch. When multitudes are standing upon the slippery edge of a precipice, a touch is sufficient to plunge them to the bottom. Grant only what Bro. Watson has granted, and there is no power in reason to resist the ultimate catastrophe; and when reason is captive to false principles we know of no means for the saving intervention of grace. '*Faith is reason leaning on God*,' and God is believed on only in his word. When another revelation is admitted as the ground of faith, inevitably it soon becomes 'another gospel,' or another guide for the soul.

"The process has been fearfully illustrated in the history of many who began only by admitting the ministry of the spirits of the dead. They necessarily learned to seek from these supposed spirits answers to the many harassing questions that disturb the religious mind. Ghosts became interpreters as well as prophets, and being only the creations of vain imaginations and disordered passions, the religion they taught became the reflection of the condition of mind and heart they represented.

"Bro. Watson began the controversy with the understanding that it was to be decided by the Word of God. Now he requires that it be decided by the Word of God, the *standards of our Church*, and the *testimony of reliable witnesses*. With all respect to Bro. Watson we must insist that in a matter involving questions of fundamental importance in religion, the decision must rest absolutely and exclusively upon the Bible. We will not consent that the opinions of Dr. Clarke, elevated above the grade of individual worth by the designation of 'standard,' shall have any more weight than they are logically entitled to. We take the liberty to dissent from his opinions in more instances than this. Bro. Watson has no right to quote all his opinions as doctrines of the Church. The Church never believed that Eve was tempted by a monkey, as the Doctor did, and has never, that we know of, consented to his doctrine of ministering ghosts.

"As to 'reliable human testimony,' of course we must rely on it. But we must find it first. The mere fact that a witness is a good man, an intelligent man, an honest man, by no means constitutes him a *reliable* witness. These qualities convince us only of the man's character, not of the truth of his impressions or conclusions. Among the victims of mesmerism and spiritism are honest and intelligent men, who assert that they see ghosts and receive messages from them, but the messages are contradictory to God's truth, or to the concurrent testimony of the whole sane world. A doctor of divinity, a man of learning, a shrewed man of business, tried to convince us of the truths of mesmerism by assuring us that a German professor had written him that he had seen a clairvoyant read a letter through a stone wall. He vouched for the honesty and intelligence of his correspondent. The human testimony was all complete, but we did not believe a word of the miracle nevertheless, because we could not admit that the testimony of one man ought to overthrow the testimony of millions to the fact that human eyes can not see through stone walls, and that human abdomens can not see at all. To convince us, the Doctor then told us how a negro boy had seen into his (the Doctor's) lungs, and described the disease there 'exactly as physicians had described it.' We promptly denied the fact, compelled him to go into particulars, and in a short cross-examination drew out the truth that the negro had described nothing as it really was.

"The testimony offered by Bro. Watson concerning 'the old clock' is utterly worthless, because the witnesses are known only to be *honest*, which is not the question. We must know more. Once, a gentleman in our parlor told us some extraordinary stories of supernatural occurrences to himself. Of course we listened in silence. When he had left, we remarked that the poor gentleman was insane. The remark startled the hearer, but in a few months the painful truth was revealed. When Bro. Watson published his first letter we said that we must know the condition of his mind, his disposition to the supernatural, before we could weigh his testimony. Since his declaration of opinions nobody can be surprised about his clock story. He believes in it, and he believes in spectral arms, and even *in the ghosts of guitars and harps retaining the power of musical vibrations* as when their tangible strings struck the resisting air. A man who can believe not only that the spirits of dead men can play the guitar for living ears, but that the spirits of guitars and harps can be played upon with material effect, can hear clocks strike whenever he is in the humor.

"That Bishop Otey was deranged before he died is certain, unless, which we have no reason to suspect, *he eat opium*, which many 'seers' undoubtedly do. The spirits seen by the sick and dying are certainly not admissible testimony. They are very common illusions, sometimes agreeable and sometimes the reverse. The subject of these hallucinations is well understood. The medical books are rich in the record of them. We knew an excellent Methodist preacher who saw horns like those of an ox on his own head—otherwise he was sane. Once he went to preach from our own door, and got into the carriage with great difficulty, putting down his head sideways and getting his horns through the door as an ox works his way into a stable. Yet he preached ably. Had he seen '*his daughter's ghost*' instead of the horns, his testimony would have been as *reliable* in the one case as in the other.

"But it is idle to follow Bro. Watson through these stories. Mere assertion proves nothing. Good character proves nothing but honesty in making the assertion. Spectral appearances are common phenomena of disordered senses. Swedenborgianism and spiritism are prevalent opinions secretly disordering the minds of thousands. Under these circumstances, mere ghost stories are of no value. But Bro. Watson has opened to us his doctrine of the spirit world, and we say, unhesitatingly, that it is unscriptural and dangerous in the extreme. Neither Bro. Watson, nor Dr. Clarke, nor any bishop, has a right to say that the spirits of the dead live about us, and commune with us, and minister to us. If they do, the Chinese are reasonable in praying to them; for no human being can talk to such spirits without telling his wants and wishes, and asking assistance, which is *prayer*. Doing this, as he inevitably must, he will rely upon their supposed communications. Believing in phantoms, he will follow fantasys. The Bible nowhere authorizes such belief. It leaves the state of the dead in profound mystery, giving consoling assurance of their rest. That they are angels or messengers, is nowhere revealed to us.

"As to 'the man who appeared to Manoah's wife,' or 'the man who appeared to Paul,' the question whether they could make an old clock strike,' is altogether irrelevant. We do not know whether they *could or not ; the question is, whether they ever did.* But we deny these were human ghosts. We have no authority to believe that they were. What have they to do with our matter?

"In conclusion, Bro. Watson earnestly denies connection with 'modern spiritualism, as it is understood.' Certainly; but he is very closely connected with it as it is *not* understood. The basis of it all is just such loose assumptions and ready confidence as Bro Watson avows. The ultimate result that he abhors is only the extreme but logical conclusions to which many as good as he have been conducted. Bro. Watson may have strength to stand where he is; but there are many for whom he writes who have not his power of resistance. Many, once convinced of the supernatural powers of old clocks and musical instruments, finding these 'phenomena' accredited by Dr. Watson, will give themselves up to the faith in the charlatans and idiots who make a trade of *divination;* for, to be plain with Bro. Watson, his 'old clock' is just an instrument of the divination which God has always forbidden and denounced."

On the receipt of this last editorial, I wrote my reply and forwarded it forthwith to the *St. Louis Christian Advocate.* It never appeared. After several weeks, the following editorial was published:

"THE MARVELOUS.

"The 'clock that struck one' was a curious story. It has been the occasion of entertaining, and, we hope, profitable disquisition upon the subject to which it relates. Dr. Watson's defence of his theory has been skillful, and has been persisted in, notwithstanding Dr. Bond's elaborate and searching criticism. We now inform the disputants that the controversy has brought to this office stories of the marvelous, enough to make a book. They have observed, also, that the attention of our correspondents have been arrested, and comments provoked. Even from across the water—from the old country—'Clericus' sends his experience and observations. This may be accepted as the conclusion of the whole matter, for the present."

This was, evidently, written by Rev. Thos. J. Finney, resident editor of the paper. He might have continued that "Clericus," his foreign correspondent referred to, made another "observation" respecting the discussion. He said that Dr. Bond could not dispose of it by writing as he had done. That he must meet it by argument, not by ridicule.

I regret the refusal to publish my reply. I think, under the rules of controversy, I had a right to claim it. If it had been done, this book would never have been published.

I had a right to expect it, from the following letter written by Dr. Bond to me, bearing date, Baltimore, July 22d, 1870 :

"DEAR BRO.—I have just received your letter, and slip inclosed. As I am about going to the mountains for a week, this will prevent my replying immediately. Of course, I will publish your letter, and reply to it, though it opens a wide field for us both. I think, with you, that it is of immense importance to settle, as far as we can, the boundary between faith and superstition. Let us, then, discuss it *fully*, *deliberately*, and thoroughly. I see that you are the kind of disputant one may safely, usefully, and agreeably encounter. You, like myself, evidently care for truth, not victory. So let us go at it. But you must wait until I get back. I have a communication from Virginia defending you.

"Yours, truly, THOS. E. BOND."

I will here give the article which was refused, that all may see the end from the beginning, so far as Dr. Bond and myself are concerned :

DR. BOND—*Dear Sir :* Your editorial of the 30th has been received, and read with surprise as well as interest. At first I thought my self-respect would not permit me to reply to it; as I had distinctly stated to you in my last, that "if you have any design to refer to modern spiritualism, as it is understood, I respectfully decline any further reply to anything you may say."

In your first paragraph you speak of "atheistic spiritism" and the wretched "jugglery of the Fox girls." The casual reader might suppose that was the subject matter of our controversy. You edit the largest of all our Church papers, and if you are disposed to write against such things have all the space you desire for that or any other purpose. I certainly can never be drawn into a defence of anything of that k nd, with you or any other person. You endeavor to identfy me with these, and try to hold me responsible for the consequences.

I will ask you Dr., is that fair? Is it in accordance with one of the plainest rules of controversy? (See rule 6th, page 161 of Hedges' Logic). "The consequences of any doctrine are not to be charged on him who maintains it, unless he expressly avows them.

If an absurd consequence be fairly deducible from any doctrine, it is rightly concluded that the doctrine itself is false; but it is not rightly concluded that he who advances it supports the absurd consequence."

Is it right then, while I am defending a Bible doctrine, believed in and advocated by Mr. Wesley, Dr. Clarke, Richard Watson, and all the writers of any note in the early history of Methodism, that I should be suspected of "atheistic spiritism," and the consequences, while I deny the premise, as well as the conclusion? Enough on the preliminary.

In your article of August 9th, you say "3d. That they do a thousand things! or any number of things as hard as the handling of the old clock, without regard to the obstruction of its case. We deny it. We know no evidence of it. The Bible gives none. Bro. Watson must give us proof." You close that editorial by saying: "We must wait for his reply to our request for the evidence upon which his statements about spirits are based." You demanded, and I felt in honor bound to give the "proof." I first gave it from the Bible. Then the opinion of our most learned commentator upon it; then the opinion of Bishops of both branches of the Church to which we belong; then of an Episcopal Bishop; lastly, one of your own profession. You repudiate them all as unreliable witnesses, and say that "Bishop Otey was deranged." I knew him well from 1838 to the time of his death, living in the same city most of the time. I visited him in his last illness, but never before heard any one hint such a thing in regard to him. The time has passed Dr. for such an argument as that.

It is said there is a peculiar state of mind that some people have who think others are deranged. If I were to find myself entertaining that opinion of others, I should certainly try to analyze my own mind to see if I were capable of forming a correct judgment of their intellectual status. I merely quoted Dr. Clarke, because of his capacity to understand the true meaning of the Scriptures equal to any one who has ever written relative to them in our Church. If he ever used the term "ministering ghosts" I never saw it, but he does use the term, St. Paul does, of "ministering spirits." As to your "Mesmerism and Clairvoyance," I know nothing, but would be pleased to have you take them off, as I know you can, in a separate article. But Dr., you must excuse me, I can neither be driven nor persuaded to follow you in your crusade against them. Neither can I stop to look at your "Methodist preacher who saw horns like an ox on his own head."

"It is idle to follow through these stories," say you. I gave you facts from as reliable witnesses as, perhaps, could be found. Testimony, upon which any court of justice would inflict capital punishment. But you say "mere assertion proves nothing." Will you be kind enough to tell me what will prove something? Does not the Bible itself rest upon testimony? Were those who lived hundreds and thousands of years ago more capable of bearing truthful testimony than men, occupying as sacred a position as they did, in this age of the world, especially when their testimony is in accordance with the declarations made by them, of what they heard and saw for themselves? Can you question that Peter and James and John were present when "Moses and Elias" appeared to and conversed with Jesus? "When the disciples heard it they fell on their face and were sore afraid."

I think it very likely that the Saducees all said, "That's only a ghost story." "Spectral appearances are common phenomena of disorded senses," as you declare in your last.

I have several times tried to get you to let our "old clock" question pass, but have failed to turn your attention to other "old clocks" which have been guilty of the same thing. You pass in silence over them, though the facts, testified to by the highest authority known in our Church, are substantially the same.

You say "For the old clock is just an instrument of the divination which God has always forbidden and denounced." Now, Dr., this is a very grave charge which I think has not the slightest foundation in truth. It is very certain that no member of my family had any agency in its striking, either of the times it struck, previous to the death of one of them each time; nor did I ever hear that any such thing had ever occurred under such circumstances. I think you must be hard pressed to make such an assertion. A few days since while I was absent in Kentucky, a gentleman of this city, whom I have known for more than thirty years, who has always entertained your opinion of these things, told me that he had an old clock that had not run or struck for years. It struck one, last week. His beloved wife died suddenly soon afterward. She was well at the time the clock struck once only. Must that deeply afflicted man whose heart is bleeding at every pore, and whose bitter tears of grief are flowing, be told that "his old clock" is just an instrument of divination which God has always forbidden and denounced? No, Dr.! such arguments will never make converts to your cause, in this age, nor check that spirit of investigation which is characteristic of the times in which we live. I would like to say more, but I fear your St. Louis editor might curtail me.

You say "Neither Bro. Watson nor Dr. Clarke nor any Bishop has a right to say that the spirits of the dead live about us and commune with us and minister to us. The Bible nowhere authorizes such belief." Now, Doctor, if you are disposed to discuss that question, and take the Bible as *the only authority*, I should be pleased to do so, and will take your own language which I have quoted for the question to be discussed. I will affirm and you deny, each having something like the same amount of space in your paper. It must be distinctly understood that we will ignore every other authority but the Bible, and confine ourselves strictly to the question as above stated. If you accept this proposition let me know at your earliest convenience. I am yours, very truly,

MEMPHIS, *Sept.* 22. 1871. SAMUEL WATSON.

About the first of March, Dr. Bond published the following Editorial:

"The *teraphim*, whatever their form, were used for divination. They were not meant to be idolatrous, but to satisfy the craving for supernatural information that God has refused to satisfy. This clinging to magic seems almost incurable; yet it is not only idle, but positively wicked, and hateful to God. It is painful to confess that, even in our days, people are found to wear amulets and charms, blessed by the clergy or manufactured by nuns, in which they trust implicitly for protection. Even Protestants seek communication with the ghosts of the dead, and imagine information of future events in the sounds of old clocks and other magical phenomena. So Micah had his *teraphim*, and yet worshiped Jehovah, as Laban and Rachel did."

TO THE PUBLIC.

When I saw the above I determined upon the course I have adopted. No one who has read our articles can doubt as to what he refers about "old clocks." I have embodied what I believed to be the truth which will ultimately prevail over error and prejudice. I can have no private or selfish purpose to subserve in thus subjecting myself to the ridicule of many with whom I have been so intimately associated. I have passed that period in life when ambition would prompt me to that kind of notoriety which will lead some to think of me as Dr. Bond has expressed himself. Having been cradled in the Methodist Church, and devoted over thirty-five years to the active work of the ministry, I have found much to strengthen my belief in her doctrines, as I understand them, from the Bible and her standard authorities. Having been refused a hearing through her organs I have been driven to the present plan of vindicating myself before an enlightened public. My self-respect as well as a sincere conviction of duty impels me to this course. I can not avoid it and satisfy my conscience as an honest man. I claim nothing for myself that I do not concede to all others,—the right to think, speak, and write independantly, if not through one, some other channel than a Methodist "*Christian Advocate.*" I do not claim the authorship of the contents of this volume, or indorse all that I have copied from various sources. Truth and error are mixed in this state of being. Every one must use the ability God has given him to separate the one from the other. The time is coming when truth will triumph and all error be banished from our mental and moral vision. I trust I have not been prompted by any motive that will not bear the scrutiny of the omniscient God.

Praying His blessings upon what may be in accordance with his will, and that all may be sanctified to the good of our common brotherhood, I am, truly yours,

SAMUEL WATSON.

TABLE OF CONTENTS.

CHAPTER I.
                                                    PAGE

Man and His Relations.................................... 35

CHAPTER II.
The Intermediate State; Place of the Departed; Bible Proofs; Samuel and Saul; Witness of Resurrection; Conclusive Evidence; Spirits' Departure; Spiritual Body; Ascension of Christ; Success of the Gospel; Delight of Spirits.......... 42

CHAPTER III.
Testimony of the Christian Fathers. Of Plato, Socrates, Pythagoras, Homer, Irenæus, Justin Martyr, Tertullian, Clement, Origen, Cyprian, Constantine; Greek Church, Roman Catholic; Melanchthon, Tillotson, Beveridge, Baxter, Dr. Hawks. 59

CHAPTER IV.
Testimony of Methodists: Mr. Wesley, Dr. Adam Clarke, Richard Watson, Dr. Wilber Fisk; Bishop McKendree and other Bishops.. 65

CHAPTER V.
Testimony of others: S. W. *Presbyterian*, Dr. Barnes, Rev. H. W. Beecher, Longfellow, Channing — Necessity for Something; Spirit Communion Meets that Need................ 73

CHAPTER VI.
First Investigations; Personal Experience; Communications to *Advocate* in 1855; Organization of Circle; Spirit Writing; Slander Refuted; Christ's Character...................... 79

CHAPTER VII.
God and Heaven; Celestial City; Providence; Intermediate State; Spirit Communion; Angels are Men................ 92

CHAPTER VIII.

The Spiritual World; Universal Law; Progression; Belief, not Universal; None have Gone to Heaven; Dr. Winans; Mental Telegraph.. 102

CHAPTER IX.

Knowledge of Spirits; Mystery's Opinion, Bacon's; Judge Edmund's Letter; Different Languages; Confession; Searching Investigation; Children; Mothers; Philosophy of Future State.. 114

CHAPTER X.

"Outer Darkness"—Trance, Nature of; Evil Spirits; Suicide; Thomas Lay; Persons Seen After Death................. 123

CHAPTER XI.

Spiritual Manifestations; Bible Proof; Law; Coming Events; Soul's Departure; Advice; Last Meeting of Circle; Bright Prospect... 133

CHAPTER XII.

Further Investigations; Communications from Mother, Mystery, Father, Andrews; Spirits Seen; Cases; Episcopal Clergyman.. 149

CHAPTER XIII.

The Philosophy and Reliability of these Manifestations; Letters; What Shall We Do? Hon. Robert Dale Owen; Moral Gravitation; Triumphs of Christianity.................... 162

CHAPTER XIV.

Communications received through Dr. J. V. Mansfield—From my father; Rev. J. D. Andrews, and Charles Scott. Second Interview—From my Wife; Wm. K. Poston, and Mrs. Lucy Leonora Winchester. Third Interview—Mollie, Bettie, Allen, Rev. John Newland Maffitt, Bishop Soule, Gen. Rivers, Rev. J. Frazer, Rev. Moses Brock, Susannah Watson. Fourth Interview—Dr. Gilbert, Dr. Seat, Bishop Otey, and Dr. Howcott, My Sister Mary, Brothers Wm. H. and John A., Mrs. Mary A. Tate, Wm. K. Poston, Bettie, Dr. Stephen Olin, Rev. Mr. Hyer, and Rev. Daniel Jones; Manner of Writing; Judge Edmund's Letter. Fifth Interview—Mollie, Wm. K. Poston, Q. C. Atkinson, Dr. Parsons. Last Interview—Mollie, Wm. K. Poston, Allen Dupree, Levin Watson, Dr. Parsons... 181

THE CLOCK STRUCK ONE.

CHAPTER I.

MAN AND HIS RELATIONS.

In Dr. Bond's last reply, to which he refuses me an answer, he distinctly says:

"Neither Bro. Watson, nor Dr. Clarke, nor any bishop, has a right to say that the spirits of the dead live about us, and commune with, and minister to us. The Bible nowhere authorizes such belief."

In reply to this, I say: "Now, Doctor, if you are disposed to discuss that question, and take the Bible as the only authority, I should be pleased to do so; and I will take your own language, which I have quoted, for the question to be discussed. I will affirm, and you deny." For reasons no doubt satisfactory to themselves, the editors declined the discussion, or even to give my article an insertion in their paper.

I now propose to show that the Bible does warrant such belief, and that it has been the doctrine of the Churches from the apostles' time.

Before entering upon the subject, let us take a view of man and his relations to this as well as the other life. Says one: "The proper study of mankind is man." What is his *origin*, his *nature*, and *ultimate destiny?* are questions of the deepest interest to all who think properly of themselves.

In order properly to understand our subject, we should analyze ourselves as far as we may be able. The Psalmist says, "I am fearfully and wonderfully made." That we have a high and holy calling, and a glorious destiny that awaits us, no one can question who has read in the Bible of man's creation, redemption, and ultimate glorification.

What does the Bible teach relative to this masterpiece of God's creation? A council is held by the Trinity before he is brought upon the stage of action. Gen. i. 26, 27: "And God said, Let us make man in our image, after our likeness. So God created man in his own image," and "breathed into his nostrils the breath of life, and man became a living soul."

Here we see his compound being composed of the animal, which is of the earth, and his soul, or spiritual nature, which God breathed into him. His material nature connects him with earth, and causes him to live in the sphere of effects. His spiritual nature connects him with, and causes him to live in, the sphere of causation. Man's physical nature or constitution is peculiarly fitted for this world. It could perform its office in no other. It is but the outer garment of the soul—a physical building for the mind while inhabiting this world, with its five windows looking out upon the world of effects.

Man's spiritual nature is exclusively his own. This spiritual nature has its peculiar constitution, which calls for things necessary for its spiritual health and development. It is a refined substance, as *real* and as *tangible* to the spiritual world as the body is to the natural world. This is what constitutes our individuality, and forms the statue of the man. This inner man, as St. Paul calls it, is to live on ever. In a qualified sense he is divine—"a son, an heir of God, and a joint heir with Christ." There is a moral dignity which the Bible stamps upon man that does not pertain to any other created intelligence. The redeemed, purified soul sustains a relation to the Divine Trinity unknown to the angels. He can commune with God, and have his "conversation in heaven."

Man in his fallen state is a creature of prejudice. His religious prejudices are, perhaps, his strongest. I know the difficulty of overcoming our religious opinions received in childhood. The impression made upon the young heart is the most permanent. We have been educated to think it was impossible for us to know anything respecting the mode of existence or action of those who have passed away from our sight. Our spiritual teachers have led us to believe that the spirit was immaterial, and that is nearly all they can tell us about it. Spiritual existence and nonentity have been to the minds of many synonymous terms.

Although men in all ages of the world have hoped for immortality, comparatively few have had such evidence as was entirely satisfactory to themselves of this important truth. The authority of past ages did not give that interior satisfaction which the earnestness and quiet of the soul require. This demand for more palpable evidence is not confined to the professedly skeptical. It is felt by many in the religious world. It may resolve to be satisfied. It may refuse to listen to the troublesome doubts which arise within. It may say with trembling, "Lord, I believe," but in its secret soul it will exclaim, "Help thou mine unbelief." That such demand for evidence exists will be admitted by a large proportion of professed believers in immortality. The spiritual aspirations of the soul are for immortality—eternal life. This is a demand of its nature, and a strong argument for its never-dying principle.

The spirit of the age demands the utmost freedom of thought and investigation in regard to those things which pertain to man's spiritual interests. The sovereignty and the equality of the individual are being universally recognized in civil matters, and the mass of mankind who are capable of thinking are disposed to comply with one precept, to "CALL NO MAN MASTER" in things pertaining to our spiritual interest and of so much moment. Authority, as a substitute for truth and right, must disappear, and everything based upon human authority alone must pass away. The Bible alone is our authority upon every subject of a spiritual nature. To its teaching we submit, and will follow wherever it may lead in the investigations we make on this occasion. Philosophy may teach us that we can not behold spiritual beings with the natural organs of sight. The Bible, as we shall show before we close, flatly contradicts this assumption of man, and demonstrates, under every dispensation, facts which come in direct conflict with this theory. Which must we believe?

Who are *the angels?* While we admit there is another form of being from the redeemed mortal who shouted for joy at the creation, yet we shall attempt to prove that many of the angels spoken of in the Scriptures were nothing more nor less than men. Here we have the position clearly stated. If it be not true that good men become angels, after they leave the body, the scores of times they are spoken of as such in the Bible is calculated to make an erroneous impression upon the minds of honest inquirers after truth. It would be clearly very improper and absurd to apply the term man, or men, to those messengers, and yet nothing is more common all through the Old and New Testaments. The name angel has respect to their office as messengers, and not to their character as beings. Whatever may be the character of the being, if he is acting as a messenger or minister, he assumes the office, and may be designated by the term angel. Hence, we have the expression angels of God; also the devil and his angels, angels of the churches, etc. The name angel does not express the character of the being. It indicates nothing respecting the nature or origin of angelic beings, except, perhaps, as usually indicating spiritual beings rather than material individualities. The name is sometimes applied to them, as in Revelation it speaks of the angels of the churches in Asia. Again, so far as I have any information or knowledge on the subject, everything indicates that the angels or spiritual messengers are disembodied human spirits. They have thoughts and affections like men. They are spiritually receptive and impartive like men. They converse like human beings, *in form, feature, and expression.* They are, in nothing hitherto perceived, to be distinguished from human beings.

So far as authority may be consulted to establish facts, the same beings are also called men in the Old and New Testaments. There is no known or apparent occasion for angels being other and different beings from the spirits of men deceased. If human beings have spiritual faculties to be addressed, those possessing like faculties can address them.

Again, there is manifest propriety in considering the spirits of human beings angels, both guardian and ministerial. From their very nature and constitution, they are best adapted to the work of guardianship and ministration, and the work is best adapted to their growth and development. Work—employment—is heaven's great law of growth, whether in the works of nature as we behold them in man's natural being, his mental nature, or his spiritual development here, and when he passes into the spiritual world of which this is a type. The kingdom of grace and the kingdom of glory are but one, differing in degree, and the great principle of action is, we think, necessary for development. Man, in the individualization of his spirit, joins upon the divine, and includes within himself the last of finite individuality. His moral dignity will never be known fully until the eternal world shall reveal it to all—when the divine image shall be stamped again upon his redeemed and glorified nature.

The question is, whether spirits of departed human beings have ever been in communication with men on earth. The belief that the spirits of human beings who have left their earthly forms have been in communication with men in the earthly form, is as universal as faith in the immortality of the soul. All the ancient doctrines of necromancy and divination attest such an opinion; and these doctrines, in one form or other, have been received and taught as verities among all nations recognizing the reality of a future life. Jews and Christians, in their sacred Scriptures, have published such communications to the world as facts not to be questioned. The fact of communication between spiritual beings and minds in the body is fundamental to all systems of religious faith. Take away from the Scriptures all the accounts of spiritual manifestations through the instrumentality of spiritual or angelic beings, and the faith of the world in the Bible, as a book of spiritual manifestations, is at an end. Those who deny the actuality or possibility of spiritual manifestations through the agency of angelic or spiritual beings, have, as we conceive, misunderstood the plainest teachings of that *blessed book*. They say, the angels are another and different class of beings from those who once lived here, and inhabited the human form. To this I can not agree, for many strong and substantial reasons, a few of which I propose to notice.

Angelic beings, mentioned under every dispensation, appear in human form, speaking the human language, exercising the faculties of the human mind, both in respect to thought, feeling, and sentiment. They seem to possess no character which does not belong to the human spirit.

They nowhere claim any different origin, and, so far as the harmony and uniformity of the divine government is concerned, it is impossible to conceive of any other method of creating or forming finite human intelligences than that which is involved in the formation of the human spirit. That angels, as individual messengers for good or for evil, are finite beings, no one will deny; that so far as they have revealed themselves, or have been revealed, to the world, they are such as human spirits are capable of becoming, is most evident. It is a permanent, living truth. Hence, to infer that angelic beings are other than the spirits of those who once inhabited the human form is as unphilosophical as it is unscriptural, as we expect to prove to a moral demonstration. That the human spirit has the capacity of the angels will hardly be denied by any who have studied man's *origin*, *history*, and *destiny*, as revealed in the Bible—man, as the son and child of the Infinite. He is begotten in the highest possible image. He is capable of coming into the highest communion—communion with God, his Father. Angels are the unfolding human spirits—those who have, under the divine government, gone before us, individualizing in their existence and perfecting their characters. They are those who commenced earlier than ourselves studying the character and work of their Father in heaven. They have laid aside their material body and have put on their spiritual body, or inner man, as St. Paul calls it. In that body they visit the abodes of men on earth, where they once lived and labored, as we are doing. There is as real and as tangible a world around us to spiritual beings as the material world is to natural beings. Matter is no obstruction to spirit; like its type, electricity, it penetrates and permeates perhaps throughout the physical universe. The empty space, as it is sometimes called, has countless myriads of living, spiritual beings, some of whom have manifested themselves to men in olden times, as we shall show from the Bible account given us.

For these and many other reasons, I affirm that the angels are the spirits of departed human beings; that it is part of their mission as angels to assist by instruction and other means the unfolding and perfecting of those who need their assistance; and this is a work of love they are performing, and that which is most needed for their own development. Whenever God has more use for his creatures in the spiritual than he has in the natural world, then they lay aside their natural body, out of which comes their spiritual body adapted to the world into which it enters. It is still engaged in carrying out the plans of the divine government in a new sphere, and with greatly increased facilities for doing the will of God in paradise as they have done in this infant, chrysalis state of being.

CHAPTER II.

THE INTERMEDIATE STATE.

The Bible, as I understand it, teaches that mankind, when they put off the clay tenement, go to what may be called the intermediate state, or paradise. They do not enter into their final abiding place, but wait, so to speak, till the affairs of this present state of existence shall have been consummated. If I recognized human opinions or authority, I could quote the highest of human authority, and say there is nothing in the Bible to warrant such belief. Says one of them:* "It is indeed very generally supposed that the souls of good men, as soon

---

* Rev. John Wesley.

as they are discharged from the body, go directly to heaven; but this opinion has not the least foundation in the oracles of God." Another, occupying the highest position known in a Protestant Church, says: "No one has ever yet been saved in heaven; no one sent to hell." Our Saviour said to the penitent thief on the cross: "This day shalt thou be with me in paradise." After his resurrection, he said to Mary: "I have not yet ascended to my Father and your Father." This state may be surrounded by several localities, known—

First. In the Scriptures as "outer darkness." Hence the influence prevailing here is called the "prince of the power of the air."

Second. A place known as one of happiness and delight, called paradise, where the good, the pure, and the true are found in their appropriate place, and become guardian angels—"ministering spirits sent forth to minister for them who shall be heirs of salvation." (Heb. i. 14.)

Third. A place wherein is found that high and exalted condition of spirit, that can perceive and realize the divine presence, not in manifestation only, but in being— where are those who have been born of the Spirit, baptized by the Holy Ghost into Christ, and have put on Christ— a place and condition called the "*Third heaven.*"

While in this present state of probation, we are fitting ourselves for the one or the other of these places. We may become allied to angels of the third heaven, or we may debase our natures to the low and degraded condition of "outer darkness," where there is weeping and wailing.

It is a beautiful, glorious truth that, under the divine government, to each man is committed the keys of the kingdom of heaven. By his own state and condition he can determine his own associations, and their influence, both here and hereafter. He makes his own place, and by the great universal law of affinity he is attracted to it. It is a fundamental principle that man is a spirit as well as an animal—his material nature mortal, his spiritual nature immortal. In speaking of his spiritual body, we do so in reference to his real life and existence, which is far above the plane of his material existence. His intellectual and moral or spiritual nature constitutes his individuality— his personality. The real man never dies. The chrysalis breaks, and the inner man passes through the veil into the spirit world identically the same he is here, with employment suited to his surroundings and desires.

BIBLE PROOFS.

I come now directly to notice some of the places where men have been seen and conversed with—persons who we belive were men who have lived here and passed away. We will cite only a few, under the patriarchal dispensation, in the times of the *Judges* and *Kings*, and the *Prophetic dispensation*, leaving the Christian dispensation for the conclusion.

Gen. xviii. 2 : Lo, three men stood by him. Abraham ran to meet them, got water, and washed their feet. He then ran into the herd, fetched a calf, tender and good, gave it to a young man, and he hastened to dress it. He told his wife to make ready quickly three measures of fine meal, and make cakes upon the hearth. And he took butter, and milk, and the calf which he had dressed, and set it before them; and he stood by them under the tree, and they did eat. The men rose up from thence and looked toward Sodom; and Abraham went with them to bring them on the way. One of these may have been our Saviour in human form, which he took to redeem us; for he says, "before Abraham was, I am." The other two came to Sodom, and talked with Lot, and warned him of the doomed cities. They urged him to flee with his family. The men laid hold of his hand, and upon the hand of his wife, and upon the hands of his daughters, saying, "Escape with thy life; look not behind; escape to the mountains, lest thou be consumed." Here are men talking with Abraham and Lot.

Judges xiii. 3: And the angel of the Lord appeared unto the woman. Then the woman came and told her husband a man of God came unto me. I asked him not whence he was; neither told me his name. Then Manoah entreated the Lord, and said, O Lord, let the man of God which thou didst send come again unto us. And God hearkened to the voice of Manoah, and the angel of God came again unto the woman as she sat in the field; but Manoah, her husband, was not with her. And the woman made haste, and ran and showed her husband, and said unto him, Behold, the man hath appeared to me that came unto me the other day. And Manoah arose and went after his wife, and came to the man and said unto him, Art thou the man that spakest unto this woman? and he said, I am.

If this man's testimony is true, he was a man who talked with the parties.

1 Sam. xxviii. 3: Now Samuel was dead, and all Israel had lamented him, and buried him. Then said the woman, Whom shall I bring up unto thee? And he said, Bring me up Samuel. And when the woman saw Samuel, Saul asked, What form is he of? and she said, An old man cometh up, and he is covered with a mantel. And Saul perceived that it was Samuel, and he stooped with his face to the ground, and bowed himself. And Samuel said to Saul, Why hast thou disquieted me, to bring me up?

Notice *prophecy: To-morrow*, etc.—*clear, indisputable, identical Samuel*, who had annointed him King of Israel.

We pass on to the prophetic dispensation.

Ezek. ix. 2: And, behold, six men came from the way

of the higher gate, and one man among them was clothed with linen; and he called to the man clothed with linen. And the Lord said unto him, Go through the midst of the city—through the midst of Jerusalem. And, behold, the man clothed with the linen, which had the inkhorn by his side, reported the matter, saying, I have done as thou hast commanded me.

Dan. viii. 13: Then I heard one saint speaking, and another saint said unto that certain saint which spake, How long shall be the vision concerning the daily sacrifice? etc. And I heard a man's voice between the banks of Ulai, which called and said, Gabriel, make this man to understand the vision.

Dan. ix. 21: Yea, while I was yet speaking in prayer, even the man Gabriel, whom I had seen in the vision. Chapter x. 5: Then I lifted up mine eyes and looked, and behold a certain man clothed in linen. . . . A hand touched me. . . . A man clothed in linen. . . . I heard the man clothed in linen, etc.

Zech. i. 8: I saw by night, and behold a man riding upon a red horse. Then said I, O, my Lord, what are these? And the angel that talked with me said unto me, I will show thee what these be. And the man that stood among the myrtle-trees answered and said, These are they whom the Lord hath sent to walk to and fro through the earth. Chapter ii.: I lifted up mine eyes again, and looked, and behold a man with a measuring line in his hand. And, behold, the angel that talked with me went forth, and another angel went out to meet him, and said unto him, Run, speak to the young man.

I might have noticed many other passages of Scripture to the same point, but I think a sufficient number have been given, even if there were no others, to demonstrate the affirmative of the proposition under every dispensation of the Old Testament.

In this history, given in the patriarchal age of the Church, we have clearly defined a principle of divine government, of the saving influence that the righteous have upon the wicked. This same principle is elaborated by the Saviour, in his Sermon on the Mount, when he said, "Ye are the salt of the earth and the light of the world." The principles of the moral government of God are the same under every dispensation. The ministry of angels is taught and exemplified under every dispensation, showing the oneness, the uniformity, of God's works and all his ways to this masterpiece of his workmanship, "made in his own image" and stamped with his own "likeness."

The persons who appeared at the resurrection of Christ are called by Matthew (xxviii. 5) "An angel answered and said unto the women, Fear not." Mark says (xvi. 5) "And entering into the sepulcher, they saw a young man sitting on the right side, clothed in a long, white garment, and they were affrighted."

Luke says (xxiv. 4, 5) "Behold, two men stood by them in shining garments. And as they were afraid, and bowed down *their* faces to the earth, they said unto them, Why seek ye the living among the dead."

John says (xx. 12) "And seeth two angels in white, sitting, the one at the head, and the other at the feet, where the body of Jesus had lain."

In these passages it is very evident that the evangelists have reference to the same beings. When they are called angels, they have reference to their office as messengers. When they are called men, they have reference to their nature as members of the same family, which Jesus came to redeem. This, to my mind, is as clear as the light of day, and is the only explanation that accords with the history and true meaning of angel as given by all commentators. It is passing strange, to my mind, that any one, with the facts before him, as revealed in the history by the evangelists, could have entertained a different opinion.

Those very persons were interested in the redemption, which had been purchased upon the cross; and the resurrection of Christ, which they had come to announce to the women, was a type and pledge of their own resurrection.

I come now to notice some of those passages where persons have appeared and conversed with persons in the flesh, where they are not called angels.

Turn to Daniel viii. 13: "Then I heard one saint speaking, and another saint said unto that certain saint which spake, How long shall be the vision concerning the daily sacrifice, and the transgression of desolation, to give both the sanctuary and the host to be trodden under foot?" Verse 16: "And I heard a man's voice between the banks of Ulai, which called, and said, Gabriel, make this man to understand the vision."

These persons are not called angels, but saints, which evidently means a sanctified human being. They were sent by God, were his messengers, and were really angels as well as saints—saints have been sent by God to converse with man, if the Bible teaches what it professes to teach—the truth. Can any one find any authority for supposing that these saints were any of the angels that shouted for joy at the creation? They were the saints who had lived here; for no other beings are ever called saints anywhere in the Old or New Testament.

See Daniel x. 5: "Then I lifted up mine eyes, and looked, and behold a certain man clothed in linen, whose loins were girded with fine gold at Uphaz." See xii. 5–7: "Then I, Daniel, looked, and, behold, there stood other two, the one on this side of the bank of the river, and the other on that side of the bank of the river. And one said to the man clothed in linen, which was upon the waters of the river, How long shall it be to the end of these wonders? And I heard the man clothed in linen, which was upon the waters of the river, when he held up his right-hand and his left-hand unto Heaven, and sware by Him that liveth forever, that it shall be for a time, times, and an half." Were these men who made these communications to Daniel in regard to such momentous events that were to occur? The Bible says they were, and it is to that alone I am to confine myself, as the only authority relative to these matters.

Having shown conclusively, as I think, to every candid mind that angel and man are used as the same person, let us now look at this subject with the light of revelation shining upon it. The Christian dead, as they are called, become angels and are sent as messengers to the living, carrying out the dispensations of God's providence and grace to the children of men. From Genesis to Revelation the Bible is filled with accounts of angels who are at work on earth. They hold sweet converse with Abraham in his tent. They are intrusted to save Lot and his family from the destruction awaiting the inhabitants of Sodom. An angel hears the wail of Hagar, who is sent out with her child, and ministers to their relief. An angel goes with Abraham's servant when he is sent to look for a wife for his son Isaac, and gives him success in his mission. The beautiful feet of an angel bring the good tidings to the maiden Mary, of the birth of the world's Redeemer. An angel directs the fleeing into Egypt, to save the young child's life. Angels minister to him and strengthen him after his temptation in the wilderness. Two of them appear and talk to him, on the Mount of Transfiguration, of the sufferings he was soon to endure at Jerusalem, to perfect the plan of human redemption. They roll away the stone from the sepulcher, and are the first witnesses of his resurrection. Two men appear at his ascension to tell the men of Galilee that this same Jesus, whom they had seen ascend, should in like manner descend again without sin unto salvation.

When the gospel is to be preached to the Gentile world, about five years after this event, one of them appeared to Cornelius while he was at Joppa, in the afternoon, and told him to send for Peter, who would show him the way of life and salvation more perfectly. When St. Paul, with Timothy, was traveling, preaching the gospel, over Asia Minor, a man from Macedonia appeared to him, and said unto him, "Come over into Macedonia and help us." Paul went immediately in compliance with the request of this native-born Macedonian, who, though a heavenly messenger, still felt an interest in the land of his nativity, and the people with whom he had been associated.

The Gospel was first preached on the continent of Europe through the agency of this man from Macedonia. This man was not plodding a quiet, lazy, half-alive, disembodied state of existence. I believe that the spirits of the just made perfect are not only cognizant of what is going on here, but that they are deeply interested in what concerns our welfare. They are not lost to us. They are only out of sight, but not far away. They loved us here, and they love us still. What we call death does not dissolve those tender ties which have bound us together. These can not be severed by the shadow of death, through which they have passed. They have left only for earth what it gave, a house in which the inhabitant lived a while. The tenant is gone out of its clay tenement, but it has carried all its consciousness; it lives, and loves, and delights to minister, as when it was mingling with those to whom it was tenderly allied.

What is more natural than that we should spend our best energies, as we spent them here, in comforting, teaching, helping, saving people, whose very souls we love better than our own? What archangel could understand

and reach the peculiarities of our nature so well as the mother who gave birth to, and nurtured her own dear children? Jesus said to his disciples, whom he loved, "Lo, I am with you always;" so I believe our loved ones are with us, when necessary, to help us in the battle of life. After that battle has been fought—as Paul said when he was confined in the prison at Rome, "I have fought a good fight,"—they hover around the dying bed, like they did around the rich man's gate, to bear away to the paradise of God the soul just emancipated from its cumbrous earth-dwelling.

The mind that guides this pen, the heart that beats in unison with loved ones here, the soul that loves God and his people, and the spirit whose aspirations are for immortality, will not, can not be affected by the change which must come over us to pass through the Valley of the Shadow of Death. We now see through a glass but darkly; there, without a dimming veil between, shall be beheld with spirit eyes this "inner man" which constitutes every one's individuality. The intellectual, moral, spiritual being, which has been using its clay tenement, has laid it aside to molder to its mother earth, while the immortal part of our being starts anew in obedience to God's plan of "ministering to those who shall be heirs of salvation."

There was a time in the history of our world when angels appeared in visible form, and freely conversed with the children of men. Their presence produced no unusual excitement or alarm. Our only source of information here is the sacred Volume. We shall, therefore, make our appeal only to this, the great storehouse of truth—alone infallible. This subject is one of the deepest interest, and should be approached divested of prejudice, and with a desire to know the truth. When we remember how often angels are mentioned in the sacred Volume—how closely related they are to God—how deeply they are interested in the plan of redemption, and how they stand identified with God's visitations both upon the righteous and the wicked—when we remember all this, surely this is fraught with importance and interest to every reflecting, intelligent mind, whatever may be his opinions. The word rendered angels signifies, both in the Hebrew and Greek languages, "messengers," and is used to denote whatever God employs to execute his purpose among the children of men.

These angels are spirits—"ministering spirits." The word angel has reference to their office, and spirit to their nature. The Hebrew, Greek, and Latin words which we render spirit, do not exactly correspond with our English word spirit. This English word spirit is opposed to matter, and designates what is immaterial. But the Greek word is not opposed to matter, but to body, and signifies not what is immaterial, but what is incorporeal. The modern idea was unknown to the ancients. In 1 Cor. xv., we are told "there is a natural body and a spiritual body." Angels, we believe, are spiritual bodies.

When in the Scriptures angels are represented as appearing with bodies in human form, no intimation is anywhere given that these bodies are not real, or that they were assumed for a time and then laid aside. It is true that the matter of these bodies was not like that of ours, inasmuch as angels could make themselves visible and vanish again from sight. But this implies no doubt of the reality of their bodies; it only intimates that they were not composed of gross matter as our bodies are. Hence, after his resurrection, Jesus often appeared to his disciples and vanished before them. Yet they never doubted that they saw the identical body of Christ, which had undergone an important change. We cannot conceive of matter, however refined, without form.

I believe that our spiritual bodies, or this "inner man," (as St. Paul calls it) is but a counterpart of our material body; that two persons passing into the spiritual world at the same time together, would recognize each other as well as to meet in the present world. This "inward man" (as it is sometimes called by the same apostle) is a substance—refined substance—as real and tangible to those in the spirit world as the body is to the material world. We cannot, we think, well conceive of this spiritual body in any other light; and with spiritual eyes we behold as real bodies in as real a spiritual world as this is a natural or material world.

Such is the extreme refinement of this spiritual body that it, like electricity, may pass through it without obstruction.

Let us compare the religious teachings of the present with those of the past, and we will find that the practical spiritualistic belief taught by the Bible has, to a great extent, been ignored in the pulpit. Ministers, for fear of being charged with being spiritualists in the modern sense of that term, have run into the other extreme, and rarely ever have the moral courage to preach on the ministry of angels and the "Communion of Saints," for fear of being charged with a belief in the ridiculous infidelity as taught by many who profess to have had intercourse with the spirits of the departed.

Nothing is more evident than that our Saviour was acting all the time in view of unseen spiritual influences, more operative to him than any of the visible and materialistic phenomena of the present life. In this respect the conduct of Christ, if imitated in the present day, would subject a man to the imputation of superstition or credulity. He imputed to the direct agency of invisible spirits, acting with affairs of life, many things. When Nathaniel, one of his early disciples, was astonished at his spiritual insight, he said to him: "Thou shalt see greater things than these. Hereafter, ye shall see heaven, and the angels of God ascending and descending on the Son of Man."

We come now to the New Testament Scriptures, which embraces the Christian dispensation. We have seen how men have appeared unto the inhabitants of earth under the patriarchal dispensation, in the time of Moses and Joshua, under the government of the Judges and Kings of Israel.

During the prophetic dispensation, they appeared unto the prophets and talked of the coming glory of the Gospel or Christian dispensation.

They open this last edition of the Gospel by appearing to the father of John the Baptist and Mary the mother of Jesus. "The man Gabriel," as he is called by Daniel, when he told him of the four great monarchies which were to precede and prepare the way for Christ's kingdom that was to be an everlasting kingdom.

It closes with the revelation made to St. John on the sea-girt isle of Patmos by one of the oldest prophets.

They appeared to the shepherds who watched their flocks by night, and announced the birth of the world's Redeemer. Their song on the occasion is the best epitome of the Gospel ever delivered to man. By their direction Joseph was warned to flee into Egypt to save the infant Saviour of the world. The great lawgiver of the Jewish nation—who never was permitted to enter the promised land, but died and was buried by God on Mount Pisgah—he appeared and talked with Jesus on the Mount of Transfiguration in Canaan. The Prophet Elijah, who went up in a chariot of fire, conversed with Jesus on that holy mountain relative to the sufferings he was to endure at Jerusalem.

When Jesus was bearing the sins of the world, in his

agony in the garden, angels ministered to him, and strengthened him for that dreadful conflict with the powers of darkness. They were the first to declare his resurrection, and the last to speak words of comfort to the men of Gallilee, who witnessed his ascension from Mount Olivet, when a cloud received him out of their sight. Who were these persons? Some may tell you they were angels. To the law and the testimony let us appeal. See Mark xvi. 5: "And entering into the sepulcher they saw a young man clothed in a long, white garment, and they were affrighted."

The youngest of the angels who shouted for joy at the creation, must have been at least four or five thousand years old at the time, and may have been several times that age. Where is then the propriety or the truth of his being called a "young man?" Can it be true that we have to resort to such interpretations of God's Word, to avoid one of the plainest and most comforting doctrines that is taught in God's holy Word. Again, Luke xxiv. 4: "And behold two men stood by Him in shining garments, and they were afraid." Neither of these evangelists call them angels but "men" and "a young man." The other two call them angels. Neither are the persons who appeared and spoke to the men of Gallilee, when Jesus ascended from Mount Olivet, even called angels, but "men." See Acts, i. 9–11. "And when he had spoken these things, while they beheld, he was taken up; and a cloud received him out of their sight. And while they looked steadfastly toward heaven, as he went up, behold, two men stood by him in white apparel, which also said: Ye men of Gallilee, why stand ye gazing up into heaven? this same Jesus which is taken up from you into heaven shall come in like manner as ye have seen him go up into heaven." Here was important conversation, in which we are deeply interested. And thus we see that while "two men" Moses and Elias, talked with Jesus about the plan of human redemption, these "two men" tell of his coming again to judge the world in righteousness.

Once more, see Rev. xxii: The angel who made the most remarkable of all the revelations, says he was one of the prophets. Who can doubt that he lived and died here, if what he says of himself be true?

Let us now return after having followed our Saviour through his life, his resurrection, ascension, and his revelation to St. John by one of the old prophets in the Isle of Patmos. We have seen that the Old Testament abounds with proofs of spiritual visitations. Noah, Abraham, Lot, and Jacob saw in vision the ladder—one foot on earth, the other reaching into heaven; and the angels ascending and descending shows that they had their origin on earth and to it descended again.

Balaam and Moses, and David and Daniel, and, in fact, nearly all the patriarchs and prophets of old, held intercourse with spirits, and talked with them face to face. The apostles received directions and held intercourse with spirits.

The Psalmist says: "The angel of the Lord encampeth around them, and delivereth them." Again, "He shall give his angels charge over thee to keep thee in all thy ways."

With these strong proofs of spirit intercourse, together with many others that might be quoted from the Scriptures, I can well say that it seems to me, from the Bible teaching, that constant intercourse existed between the two worlds in the history of our race, as given by the inspired writers. It appears to have been the most universal of all convictions. The veil between them and the invisible world must have been slight indeed. It was no matter of dread or bewilderment to them if, in the stillness of the sunset hour, stranger feet drew near their dwelling, and the phenomena of both worlds became blended into the vision. Forms, glorious with the majesty of holiness, entered their presence to have intercourse with, and teach them, in their departing, that they had been with beings of another land. The very absence of fear or wonder, in most cases, implies the original universality of such intercourse between the inhabitants of both worlds. The separation between the living and the departed was held to have been marvelously slight.

Peter first preached to the Gentiles the unsearchable riches of Christ through the instrumentality of "a man" who was interested in the Gospel. While Cornelius was at prayer, in the ninth hour, as he says, "I prayed in my house, and behold, a man stood before me in bright clothing, and said, 'Cornelius, thy prayer is heard; send, therefore, to Joppa, and call hither a man whose surname is Peter, who, when he cometh, shall speak unto thee.'" Peter comes—preaches—the spirit is poured out on the Gentiles, when Peter declares he "now perceives of a truth, that God is no respecter of persons." Again, Acts xvi. 9: And a man appeared to Paul in the night. "There stood a man of Macedonia, and prayed him, saying: 'Come over into Macedonia and help us.'" Paul went immediately to Macedonia, "assuredly gathering that the Lord had called us to preach the Gospel to them." There are two points to which I wish to call your special attention:

1. This "man" was from Macedonia. It was his native country—born there.

2. He still feels a deep interest for that, his native land, and desires Paul to preach the Gospel to them.

Macedonia was a kingdom of Greece. Alexander the Great, son of Philip, king of Macedon, having conquered Asia, and subverted the Persian Empire, the name of the Macedonians became very famous throughout the East, and it is often given to the Greeks, the successors of

Alexander in the monarchy. The apostle did not doubt his call to preach the gospel there, after this "man" appeared to him, and invited him over to his country. He was very successful over there among those Macedonians. There he laid the foundation of the church of Thessalonica and Philippi. To each of these churches he wrote Epistles in the New Testament.

What stronger proof could any one desire than is furnished by this case? This being is never called an angel, but a "man of Macedonia."

Whenever there is a demand for the Gospel in this age, it is called "the Macedonian cry." That man knew Paul was capable of preaching to those proud, intellectual Grecians; hence, he preferred him to any other of the apostles. "Greek could meet Greek" there, as he did on other occasions.

What we call death removes the chrysalis state of our material body, and opens, like the worm when the beautiful butterfly soars away with wings adapted to the atmosphere, to extract sweets from the opening flowers. To the pure, spiritual beings, there is a medium of communication far surpassing our ocean telegraphs. The atmosphere, doubtless, possesses the property of telegraphing with spirits who occupy the same plane, that will astonish us more than this type of angelic communication did when it was first discovered. Space itself may be annihilated, and with an angel's ken we may behold, not through a glass darkly, as we now do spiritual things, but with clearest vision, as one of our hymns expresses it,

"Then shall I see, and hear, and know,
All I desire or wish below,
And every power find sweet employ,
In that eternal world of joy."

The Apostle Paul, speaking of angelic spirits, says: "Are they not all ministering spirits, sent forth to minister to them who shall be heirs of salvation?"

In this passage we are expressly taught that assisting man, or communication with mankind, is not only a standing employment, or office, of angelic spirits, but that it is their only authorized use or office. Their duty and their delight is assistance, in some-mode, to those who are to be heirs of salvation. This is not spoken of as a special or isolated case—but the universal duty and privilege of all. It is the established law of the spirit land. No man living here was ever better qualified to judge of this matter than was St. Paul. He affirms that he was caught up into the "third heaven," and had an opportunity of speaking from experience. He saw and heard things unlawful to be revealed; but this was not one of them. This was a universally acknowledged fact, well known and understood there His testimony is not, therefore, to be slightly esteemed, nor invalidated by a doubt. His own history, as recorded in the Acts of the Apostles, bears his testimony to his having been thus ministered to by them.

CHAPTER III.

TESTIMONY OF THE CHRISTIAN FATHERS.

HAVING, as I think, proven from the Bible the position which I have been defending, I now proceed to give the opinion of those who lived in olden time, and in the early days of Christianity. Through all the palmy days of Egypt's grandeur this was the universal belief among the wise and profound: That "the earth was surrounded by aerial circles of ether, and that in these ether regions the souls of the dead lived and guarded mortals." Hermas taught "that the visible is but the picture of the invisible world." Ancient Greece entertained opinions nearly the same as those of modern times, of "controlling or guardian spirits." Plato says that between God and man are the darmenes, or spirits who are always near us, though commonly invisible to us, and know all our thoughts." Socrates, being inquired of why he busied himself so much in private, and did not appear in the conventions of the people, gave the following reasons: "The thing that hindered me from doing so, Athenians, was this familiar spirit, this divine voice that you have often heard of, and which Miletus has endeavored so much to ridicule. This spirit has stood by me from my infancy. It is a voice that does not speak but when it means to take me off from some resolution."

Mr. Wesley quotes Socrates in his sermon on "Good Angels," and I quote him, to show his opinion on this subject. It seems ridicule was a weapon used in ancient as well as in modern times. Socrates commenced his forty-third chapter on the theology of Plato thus: "Let us speak concerning the demons who attend the superintendance of mankind. The most perfect souls choose a life conformable to their presiding god, and live according to a divine demon." This opinion prevails throughout Grecian history. They believed in the appearance of *angels, spirits, visions,* and *trances.* To the clear vision of the Grecian, dying was ascending to the soul's primal home—the society of the celestial gods, in the starry regions of measureless space. Pythagoras professed to visit the spiritual world, and hold converse with the departed spirits, and described the condition of Homer, Hesiod, and others there.

We come now to notice the opinion of those who are quoted in regard to other matters next in authenticity to the Scriptures—the Christian Fathers, who lived near the Apostolic day.

Ignatius, Bishop of Antioch, where the disciples were

first called Christians, a loved and prominent disciple of the Apostle John, is said to have been one of the little children whom Jesus took in his arms and blessed. The Church Fathers record the fact, that in youth he was "so innocent he could hear the angels sing. This heavenly music so impressed his mind that, when becoming a bishop, he introduced into his lithurgal service the practice of singing in responses, just as he had heard in his youthful years the melodies of immortal choirs." It seems, then, that ancient as well as modern bishops believed in "spiritual manifestations." *Irenœus, Justin Martyr, Tertullian, Clement, Origen, Cyprian*, and others, represent the continuous spiritual gifts in the church. Tertullian, son of a Roman centurion, at Carthage, A. D. 160, says: "We had a right to expect, after what was said by St. John, to anticipate these spiritual gifts. There is a sister among us who possesses a faculty of revelation, commonly, during religious service. She falls into a trance, holding then communion with the angels—hearing divine mysteries explained. She declared she had seen a soul in bodily shape, that appeared to be a spirit neither empty nor formless, but so real and substantial that it might be touched. It was tinder shining, of the color of the air, but in everything resembling the human form."

Hermas, brother to Pius, a bishop of Rome, wrote his "Pater" about the middle of the second century. He relates that he saw six young men, "or, rather, angels, clothed in shining vestures, building a tower of square white stones," symbolical of the church militant. A writer in "Appleton's Biographical Cyclopedia," edited by the Rev. Dr. F. L. Hawks, speaking of this book, remarks, "that it is further interesting because offering evidence that the early Christians believed in the ministration of angels around them."

Constantine, having espoused Christianity, and being

menaced in consequence by its enemies, was compelled to take up arms for self-defence. Eusebius states that he heard Constantine declare, under oath, that when he was going to attack the tyrant, Maxentius, and was full of doubt, as he was resting in the middle of the day, and his soldiers about him, he and all his soldiers saw a luminous cross in the heavens, attended by a troop of angels, who said, " O, Constantine, by this go forth to victory."

The Greek Church of Russia, receiving her apostolic priesthood from Greece, has carefully maintained the integrity of the primitive church, with less innovation than the Roman Catholic, and is, therefore, more authoritative in respect to what the Apostolic Fathers taught. The doctrine of ministering spirits is plainly set forth in their religious histories. St. Bernard thus alludes to the divine care over us :

" We owe to our guardian angels great reverence, devotion, and confidence. Penetrated with awe, walk always with circumspection, remembering the presence of angels to whom you are given in charge, in all your ways. In every apartment, in every closet, in every corner, pay respect to your angel. Dare you do before him what you dare not commit if I saw you ? "

The Roman Catholic Church never lost the cynosure star—the ministry of angels. As her devotees have said, " We believe in the communion with saints." The second day of October is the Feast of Angel Guardians, in commemoration of spiritual commerce between us on earth and his holy angels, whose companions we hope one day to be in the kingdom of his glory.

The following are the prayers of the Roman Catholic Church, copied from their book :

"PRAYER TO OUR GUARDIAN ANGEL.

" O, Holy Angel, whom God, by the effect of his goodness, and the tender regard for my welfare, hath charged with the care of my conduct, and who doth assist me in all my wants, and comfort me in all my afflictions; who supporteth me when I am discouraged, and continually obtaineth for me new favors, I return thee profound thanks, and conjure thee most amiably, Protector, to continue thy charitable care and defence of me against the malignant attacks of my enemies. Keep me at a distance from all occasions of sin. Obtain for me the grace of hearkening attentively to thy holy inspirations, and of faithfully reducing them to practice. Protect me in all the temptations and trials of this life, but more especially at the time of my death; and do not quit me until thou hast conducted me into the presence of my Creator, in the mansions of everlasting happiness. Amen.—*Page* 639.

"TO THE ANGEL GUARDIAN.

"While we give thanks to God for having granted to each of us a holy angel for our guardian, we ought ever to bear in mind the respect, devotion, and loving confidence we ever owe that blessed spirit.

'" Angel of God, my Guardian dear,
To whom his law commits me here,
Ever this day be at my side,
To light and guard, to rule and guide,"'

Phillip Melanchthon, more spiritual in his organization than Luther, had a more equally balanced faith in the ministry of spirits, and relates several instances of such interposition in times of peril. He tells us he had seen specters (spirits), and that he knew many men worthy of credit who had not only seen, but had likewise discoursed with them.

Bishop Hall had the moral courage to vindicate this doctrine in the Protestant Church. He wrote a valuable work on "The Invisible World." He often invoked the aid of guardian spirits. He felt their continued presence, and was so impressed with high purposes to "walk carefully but confidently." In his spiritual treatise he says "So sure as we see men, so sure are we that holy men have seen angels. Have we not had intuitive intimations of the death of absent friends, which no human intelligence had bidden us to suspect? Who, but our angels have wrought it?"

Archbishop Tillotson, a great light in the English Church, speaking of the continued intercourse of angels with men, for their protection and advantage, says, "they are God's great ministers here below."

Bishop Beveridge supports the reality of ministering spirits, and says that "spirits assume a bodiless shape."

Richard Baxter, in his "Historical Discourses on Apparitions," writes an account of an acquaintance of his, "a gentleman of considerable rank, who was addicted to intemperance, and was always visited by a spirit after he had slept himself sober, warning him of his vice, by rapping on his head-board, and visible signs of heavenly guardianship and discipline." Mr. Baxter, having seen the man, besought him to reform; and believing the spirit presence to be genuine, consciously and feelingly asks, "Do good spirits dwell so near us? or are they sent on such messages? or is it his guardian angel?"

I might quote several times as much from those pious men of olden time; but enough has been given to show that it was the general belief in the earlier and purer days of Christianity, as well as of the best men of the Reformation.

CHAPTER IV.

TESTIMONY OF METHODISTS.

Mr. Wesley had unquestionable evidence of mysterious agencies, and spirit manifestations. He was personally blessed with some gifts, promised to believers. All through his evangelizing career he noted and recorded cases of spirit power, and premonition. In his journals and the "Armenian Magazine," some of the clearest cases on record will be found. In his journal—to mention only one : A lady was awaked at night by what purported to be her brother, who told her he had died that night on board a certain ship at sea, in such a latitude and longitude. A record was made that night of it, and, months after, the facts were ascertained to be as the apparition stated.

Again, he says: "Suppose my spirit was out of the body, could not an angel see my thoughts, even without my uttering any words ? (if words are used in the world of spirts). And can not that ministering spirit see them just as well now I am in the body ? It seems, therefore, to be an unquestionable truth (although perhaps not commonly observed) that angels know not only the words and actions, but also the thoughts of those to whom they minister. And indeed, without this knowledge they would be very illy qualified to perform the various parts of their ministry. And if our eyes were opened, we should see 'They are more that are for us than they that are against us.' We should see

"'A convoy attends,
A ministering host of invisible friends.'

"In all ages he [God] used the ministry both of men and angels."

This is what the founder of Methodism says upon this

subject, yet many of his sons, professing to be wise above what is written, will sneer at any demonstration of this doctrine, and talk of "morbid brain" and "superstitious turn of mind." O shame, where is thy blush!

Hear what one of the best women that ever lived says of him and the subject: " It appears to me no way contrary to reason to believe that the happy departed spirits see and know all they would wish, and are divinely permitted to know. In this, Mr. Wesley (the founder of Methodism) is of the same mind,—and that they *are* concerned for the dear fellow-pilgrims whom they have left behind. I can not but believe they are. .... Nor doth it seem contrary to reason to suppose a spirit in glory can turn his eye with as much ease, and look on any object below, as a mother can look through a window, and see the actions of her children in the court underneath it. If bodies have a language by which they can convey their thoughts to each other, though sometimes at a distance, have spirits no language, think you, by which they can converse with our spirits, and, by impressions on the mind, speak to us as easily as before they did by tongue? And what can interrupt either the presence, communication, or sight of a spirit?

" 'Walls within walls no more its passage bar
Than unopposing space of liquid air.'

"Though it is allowed we may have communion with angels, various are the objections raised against the belief of our communion with that other part of the heavenly family,—*the disembodied spirits of the just*. If there is joy throughout all the realms above, yea, 'more joy over one sinner that repenteth than over the ninety and nine, that went not astray,' how evident it is to an impartial eye that the state, both of one and the other, must be known there, together with the progress of each individual . . . Have not spirits faculties suited to spirits, by which we may suppose they can as easily discern our souls as we could discern their bodies when they were in the same state as ourselves? . . . If he maketh his angels spirits, and his ministers a flame of fire, can not a spirit be with me in a moment, as easily as a stroke from an electrical-machine can convey the fire, for many miles, in one moment, through thousands of bodies, if properly linked together?"—*Mrs. Mary Fletcher.*

Dr. Adam Clarke I have already quoted. (See his commentary, page 299, vol. XI.)

1. "I believe there is a supernatural and spiritual world in which human spirits, both good and bad, live in a state of consciousness."

2. "I believe that any of these spirits, may, according to the order of God, in the laws of their place of residence, have intercourse with this world, and become visible to mortals."

These are unequivocal expressions of belief. If, as Dr. Clarke affirms with reason, Samuel "actually appeared unto Saul," if the ascended Moses and Elias "talked with Jesus" in the presence of Peter, James and John, if spiritual beings denominated "angels" "men of God," *men*, held intercourse with the earth's inhabitants during several thousand years of scriptural history, why not now? Is God mutable? Have Deific laws changed? Has the door John saw opened in heaven been shut and barred?

The real and living verity of the future life, and spirit world, is a doctrine which can apppeal confidently to the Bible, to history, and to science, for its substantial proof, and reasonable confirmation. It is not only taught in the Bible, but proven by the concurrent testimony of every race of mankind, in all ages of the world.

I find the following in the *Lynchburg Virginian* recently. The family with whom I reside were familiar with the facts as here stated. The editor says, "We copy an account of an occurrence well remembered by some of our citizens:

"SMITH CRADLE ROCKING.

"This is one of the most remarkable and best authenticated phenomena of its kind on record. It occurred in 1840, in Lynchburg, at the residence of the late William A. Smith, D.D., for many years President of Randolph Macon College. In that year he was pastor of Lynchburg church. An empty cradle in his house was noticed rocking of its own accord. It continued its motion for an hour. The next day it comenced rocking at the same time, kept it up and stopped as on the day before. Thus it continued daily for over a month. Many intelligent citizens and ministers witnessed this wonderful affair and made repeated efforts to solve the mystery without success. It was moved to different parts of the room without any change in its behavior. It was removed to other apartments in the dwelling with the same result. It was taken to pieces and each part scrutinized and refitted, yet there was no change in its motion.

"The Methodist clergy selected one of their number to hold the cradle, and prevent, if possible, its movement. The Rev. Dr. Penn, one of the purest men of his time, was chosen for this purpose. While it was rocking he grasped it. It wrenched itself, from his grasp! He seized it more firmly. The timbers cracked and the cradle would have been broken in the struggle to release itself, had he not loosened his hold.

"It was not further hindered in its daily exercise. After thirty or more days it stopped, and never commenced again.

"No explanation of this wonderful affair was ever given or attempted."

I would respectfully ask Dr. Bond, if the physical force

used on this occasion, was not sufficient to make a "clock strike one?"

Richard Watson, of England, who was perhaps the most intellectual man the Methodist Church ever had, speaking of the case of Samuel, says: "The account not only shows that the Jews believed in the doctrine of apparitions, but that in fact, such an appearance on this occasion did actually occur; which answers all the objections which were ever raised or can be raised, from the philosophy of the case, against the possibility of the appearance of departed spirits." "I believe in this apparition of the departed Samuel, because the text positively calls the appearance Samuel."

Let us see what Dr. Watson says on this subject in his "Theological Institutes," a standard work embraced in the course of study for ministers of the Methodist Church.

"This is the doctrine of revelation; and if the evidences of that revelation can be disproved, it may be rejected; if not, it must be admitted, whether any argumentive proof can be offered in its favor or not. That it is not *unreasonable* may be first established.

"That God, who made us, and who is a pure spirit, can not have immediate access to our thoughts, our affections, and our will, it would certainly be much more reasonable to deny than to admit; and if the great and universal Spirit possesses this power, every *physical* objection, at least, to the doctrine in question is removed, and finite, unbodied spirits may have the same *kind* of access to the mind of man, though not in so perfect and intimate *degree*. Before any natural impossibility can be urged against this intercourse of spirit with spirit, we must know what no philosopher, however deep his researches into the courses of the phenomena of the mind, has ever professed to know —the laws of perception, memory, and association. We can suggest thoughts and reasons to each other and thus mutually influence our wills and affections.

"We employ, for this purpose, the *media* of signs and words; but to contend that these are the only *media* through which thought can be conveyed to thought, or that spiritual beings cannot produce the same effects *immediately*, is to found an objection wholly upon our ignorance. All the reason which the case, considered in itself, affords, is certainly in favor of this opinion. We have access to each other's minds; *we* can suggest thoughts, raise affections, influence the wills of others; and analogy, therefore, favors the conclusion that, though by different and latent means, unbodied spirits have the same access to each other, and to us."

Mr. Watson relates one of the most remarkable instances of persons returning that I ever read outside of the Bible. It was published in the *Methodist Magazine* when I was a boy, and republished in the *Methodist Magazine*, at Baltimore, a few years since. There was a man and his wife, by the name of James, both of whom died very suddenly, as was supposed, without a will. There arose serious difficulty among the heirs about the property. James and his wife came back (in the day-time) and informed a lady where the will was in a secret drawer, in a secretary. She informed the circuit preacher (a Mr. Mills), who went and found the will, and reconciled the parties.

It is too long to copy; I merely mention it to show his opinion of such things.

Bishop Simpson said, after he lost his boy, that "it seemed to him as though he were walking on one side of the veil, and his son on the other. It is only a veil. These friends will be the first to greet you—their faces the first to flash upon you, as you pass into the invisible world. This takes away the fear of death. Departed spirits are not far above the earth, in some distant clime, but right upon the confines of this world"

DR. WILBER FISK'S TESTIMONY.

"God," he says, "has use or employment for all the creatures he has made—for every saint on earth, for every angel in heaven. He would that none be idle. He has a mission for every one. Angels and archangels, cherubims and seraphims, patriarchs and prophets, apostles and reformers, and all the holy hosts of heaven, are his ministering spirits, frequently dispatched to minister unto the strangers and sojourners of earth. He sends forth these spirits to guide and guard his contrite children through this wilderness world, to their promised place at his right hand.

"Oh! consoling doctrine! Angels are around us. The spirits of the departed good encamp about our pathway. Who knows how many times the sainted spirit of Paul has been our guardian angel, protecting and defending us? Who can tell how often Marah's humble spirit has surrounded our thorny pathway, strewing it with heavenly flowers, and the golden fruits of the true life, and perfuming the atmosphere we breathe with celestial fragrance?

"Who knows how frequently the sainted spirits of Benson, and Watson, and Clarke, have hovered over our minds, directing them to the sound doctrines of the Gospel of Truth? and how often has the fervent spirit of Wesley inspired us with zeal, and the spirit of Luther with holy boldness, to contend earnestly for the faith once delivered to the saints? And how often has Bunyan's blessed spirit lingered around our path, to lead us on to God? And who knows, brethren, but it is the inspiring spirit of the flaming Whitefield, or Hall, or Chalmers, that sometimes sets on fire our stammering tongues with heavenly eloquence?"

Did not Bishop McKendree see and recognize those who were around his dying bed, when he said:

> "Bright angels are from glory come—
> They are around my bed,
> They are in my room,
> They wait to waft my spirit home."

Hear what one of our living bishops says:

"We labor not only in the sight of mortals; we labor also in the sight of celestial beings. We preach to two congregations at the same moment—one below, the other above us. Methinks they are present with us now. Poised upon celestial pinions, they shed over us the odors of paradise. I seem to hear the rustling of their plumes. The air about us is full of fragrance. Their benevolent countenances beam with delight, and their eyes, sparkling with supernatural intelligence, are watching to catch, before we disperse, another proof of 'the manifold wisdom of God.' To use the impassioned strain of a familiar hymn:

> "'Angels now are hov'ring round us,
> Unperceived they mix the throng,
> Wond'ring at the love that crown'd us,
> Glad to join the holy song.'

See "Union Pulpit," page 446.

I not only fully endorse the above quotations, but will add that, if we had our minds and affections elevated to the plane occupied by those spirits, that we could commune with them, and realize that there was indeed but a veil between those who have passed over, and those who yet tabernacle in their clay tenement. We are too earthly, if not sensual, to comprehend, appreciate, and enjoy "the communion of saints." As we arise in our moral status, we will find that we approximate those who have passed the veil; and we believe the time will come when fellowship with the Church triumphant, and the Church militant, will be realized by all who are in a condition, spiritually, to enjoy such "conversation in Heaven."

CHAPTER V.

TESTIMONY OF OTHERS.

JUST as I am writing this, I find the following in the *South-Western Presbyterian*, published at New Orleans, March '72. The writer, speaking of a case where the dying person saw his departed friends around him, says: "Does not this case, with its simple explanation, go far to unravel the mysterious incidents of many a dying experience? Those seraphic smiles playing over the face, like the sheet-lightning that sports upon a summer cloud—those typical gestures, pointing as if to some real presence, which the natural eye is unable to discern—the joyful recognition of beautiful spirits, who seem to beckon the departing soul toward the glory that is beyond: all these things so often occurring and throwing such awe upon the living, as pregnant hints of the eternity that at other times seems so far away—may they not all be only the natural expressions of spiritual desires and affections wrought in the heart by the Holy Spirit in the hour when his work is finished on the human soul? May they not be the simple reflection of the grace that is wrought within the believer, when he is made 'meet for the saints inheritance in light?' And may it not be lawful to conclude that these cases, which seem to us so rare, are but types of all the rest?" Such cases are not so "rare" as many suppose. I was called to visit a physician who was a Presbyterian Elder recently. He bore the same testimony and seemed to be astonished that all who were in the room did not see the loved ones as he did. His natural eyes were becoming dim but his spiritual eyes were being opened.

REV. DR. A. BARNES TESTIMONY.

"In this doctrine (the ministry of spirits) there is nothing absurd. It is no more impossible that angels should be employed to aid men than that one man should aid another, certainly not as impossible as that the Son of God should come down not to be ministerd unto, but to minister. Angelic ministration constitutes the beauty of the moral arrangements on earth. Is there any impropriety in supposing that they do now what the Bible says they have ever done."

The author of these sentiments made the Scriptures his study and wrote a commentary upon them. I might multiply authorities from this scource but enough has been given to answer our purpose.

REV. H. W. BEECHER'S TESTIMONY.

"I confess to you, there is something in my mind of sublimity in the idea that the world is full of spirits, good and evil, who are pursuing their various errands, and that the little that we can see with these bats' eyes of ours, the little that we can decipher with these imperfect senses, is not the whole of the reading of those vast pages of that great volume which God has written. There is in the lore of God more than our philosophy has ever dreamed of.

"On the other hand, I believe that there are angels of light, spirits of the blessed, ministers of God, I believe, not only that they are our natural guardians, and friends, and teachers, and influencers, but, also, that they are natural antagonists of evil spirits. In other words, I believe that the great realm of life goes on without the body very much as it does with the body. And, as here the mother not only is the guardian of her children whom she loves, but foresees that bad associates and evil influences threaten them, and draws them back and shields them from impending danger, so ministering spirits not only minister to us the divinest tendencies, the purest tastes, the noblest thoughts and feelings, but, perceiving our adversaries, caution us against them and assail them and drive them away from us.

"There have been times in which I declare to you heaven was more real than earth; in which my children that were gone spoke more plainly to me than my children that were with me; in which the blessed estate of the spirits of just men made perfect in heaven, seemed more real and near to me than the estate of any just man upon earth.

"These are experiences that link one with another and a higher life. They are generally not continuous, but occasional openings through which we look into the other world . . . .

"These glimpses of the future state are a great comfort and consolation to all those who are looking and waiting for that development of perfect manhood."

LONGFELLOW'S TESTIMONY.

"Some men there are—I have known such—who think
That the two worlds—the seen and the unseen,
The world of matter and the world of spirit—
Are like the hemispheres upon our maps,
And touch each other only at a point ;
But these two worlds are not divided thus,
Save for the purpose of common speech ;
They form one globe, in which the parted seas
All flow together, and are intermingled,
While the great continents remain distinct.

" The spiritual world
Lies all about us, and its avenues
Are open to the unseen feet of Phantoms
That come and go, and we perceive them not,
Save by their influence; or when, at times,
A most mysterious Providence permits them
To manifest themselves to mortal eyes.

"A drowsiness is stealing over me
  Which is not sleep; for, though I close mine eyes,
I am awake, and in another world;
Dim faces of the dead and of the absent
Come floating up before me.

"When the hours of day are numbered,
  And the voices of the night
Wake the better soul, that slumbered,
  To a holy calm delight,
Ere' the evening lamps are lighted,
  And, like Phantoms grim and tall,
Shadows from the fitful firelight,
  Dance upon the parlor wall,—

"Then the forms of the departed
  Enter at the open door—
The beloved ones, the true hearted,
  Come to visit me once more;
And with them the Being Beauteous
  Who unto my youth was given,
More than all things else, to love me,
  And is now a saint in heaven.

"With a slow and noiseless footstep
  Comes that messenger divine,
Takes the vacant chair beside me,
  Lays her gentle hand in mine;
And she sits and gazes at me
  With those deep and tender eyes,
Like the stars, so still and saint-like,
  Looking downward from the skies."

I could give the testimony of hundreds of the most intellectual and pious men that ever lived, who believed this doctrine. One more will suffice for the present.

OPINION OF REV. WILLIAM E. CHANNING.

We need not doubt the fact that angels, whose home is in heaven, visit our earth and bear part in our transactions; and we have good reason to believe that, if we obtain admission into heaven, we shall still have opportunity, not only to return to earth, but to view the operations of God in distant spheres, and be his ministers in other worlds.

Having proven, as I think, that the doctrine of intercourse between the natural and spiritual world is clearly taught in the Bible under every dispensation, and having shown it to have been the belief of the early Christians, as well as the Churches of the present time, the question now is, Can it be demonstrated that communications are now being made? I take the affirmative of this question. It is, as I conceive, but one step further than the universal belief of the Church in all ages. Before giving the reasons for my belief, it may be well to inquire, Is there not a necessity for something more tangible than the world has had of immortality? Is it not true that the pursuit of science has a materializing influence over a large portion of those who are engaged in such studies? Does not the human mind require to be moved by far different powers than those which rule the world of thought at the present time? Science tends to make men selfish and calculating, while religious dogmatism takes them further and further from the true and simple grounds of faith. Is there not a necessity for a return, on the part of the Churches, to the belief of the earliest Christians in direct and undisputed spirit communion, and that it should not be regarded as at all miraculous in its nature, but a matter of ordinary experience and the sure evidence of religious faith? The world confesses to the same thing on every side. Almost everywhere is to be found a deadness of faith, and profession without practical belief. I know that faith is powerful in its influence on the soul; but the time has come when even faith must be strengthened and re-enforced by actual knowledge. This want has been fully met in my own case for nearly a score of years. It has supplied that knowledge which I so much desired, and given vital efficacy to my faith, which nothing else could have done.

This comes, too, at the time it is most needed. Its office is to redeem mankind, who are blinded by materialism. To deny the return of persons who once lived here would, in my opinion, give to the Jewish dispensation the advantage over the Christian in this matter. There has been a gradual unfolding of the plans and purposes of God from the patriarchal age to the present. I believe that he designs this to be the means by which the last vestige of materialistic infidelity is to be driven from the world, and to greatly facilitate the time when the knowledge and glory of God shall cover the earth, and all flesh together see and rejoice in the salvation provided for the whole human family. I believe there is one simple truth to be demonstrated by these things; that is, man's immortality. No new revelation, no new doctrine or principle relative to the relation between the Creator and the creature is designed by these things. Therefore, those who rely upon what they may have received as coming from spirits teaching anything contrary to the Bible are deceived. This is what I have always been taught, and is what I most sincerely believe. I can not question the phenomena any more than I can any other facts of which my senses are capable of *judging*. There is, perhaps, as great a diversity of opinion in regard to some things in the spiritual as in the material world. Nor could I believe what comes from the former as readily as from the latter.

With these views, I give the facts which have come under my observation, leaving each one to exercise his judgment from the stand-point he may occupy, praying the blessing of God on all who may attach enough importance to them to read what is written, and the guidance of the Holy Spirit to enable them to arrive at the truth.

CHAPTER VI.

FIRST INVESTIGATIONS.

HAVING disposed of the subject-matter about which Dr. Bond and myself have written, I feel it due to truth to give some of the reasons which have led me to the conclusions at which I have arrived.

I was brought up after the strictest sect—a Methodist. My father, for about forty years, was a class-leader; hence I was cradled in this Church. In early life I trust I consecrated my heart to God and the Church. In 1836 I was received on probation in the Tennessee Annual Conference. My first year was spent on the Wayne circuit; my second on Franklin, Ala.; my third in Clarksville, Tenn. From this station I was sent to Memphis, in 1839, where I have been officially, in the city and vicinity, ever since. My prejudices were, perhaps, as strong as those of most persons against what was called "spirit-rappings." I read everything I saw against them, and I verily believed it to be one of the vilest humbugs from the land of "isms."

In 1854 our attention was arrested by noises, mostly like the knocking at a door in my house for admittance. They would occur during the day, heard by all the family, but mostly at night, in our bedroom. It became a source of great annoyance to me, but how to get rid of it was beyond my knowledge. A servant girl, who was born in our family, and had nursed three of our children who had died, said "it was the children." She said they were with her often; that she saw them and talked to them, as she did when they were living. I did not believe her, and threatened her if she persisted in such foolish notions.

One evening I had her sit down by a small table, my wife and myself only being present. Very soon there were raps on the back of my chair. I could feel the vibrations of the chair against my back. I was convinced that if they were made by the girl, it was in a manner of which I was wholly ignorant. I was perplexed, and knew not what to say or do. I resolved not to threaten to chastise her any more, or ridicule the subject as I had done. The raps continued, not only in the house, but on my person, by day and night, for months. The noise made on my shirt bosom resembled more the telegraph-machine than anything else.

It has been my custom, most of my life, to spend some portion of the evening in private devotion, meditation, and self-examination. Having read in my boyhood "Baxter's Saints' Rest," I resolved to adopt his plan of spending the close of the day in self-examination and religious exercises. I have often, when thus retired from mortal eyes, with my door locked, felt as sensibly the presence of persons as occular demonstration could have made them. These were not only as impressive, mentally and morally, but physically, as I ever felt the touch of mortals upon my person. This I know, as well as I can know any physical phenomenon. At first it produced some excitement, and even fear; but I was soon satisfied that they were those who loved me, and came to "minister" to me. It produced then the most hallowed influence upon my mind and heart, such as I never before experienced.

There was at this time much excitement on the subject of "circles" and what occurred at them in the city. I never attended any of them, nor would my self-respect permit me to be associated with what I heard occurred at them. Miss Mary, daughter of Rev. William McMahon, spent a night with us. She told us that she had never been where there was any investigation of this subject, but that when she took a pen or pencil in her hand, and sat down quietly, with paper, it would write without her agency; that she "had written in fifty different handwritings, a number of which had been compared with those by whom they professed to have been written—members of her father's and mother's family, who had long since been dead, and that they were the same chirography." After supper, while we were conversing upon the subject around the table, a rap, as loud as if struck with a hammer, was made on it. A pencil and paper were brought. I asked quite a number of questions mentally, and answers were given, demonstrating that whatever controlled the pencil was cognizant of what was passing through my mind. So far as I know, the answers were truthfully written. This was the first time I had thought of my mother in connection with this subject. She died, when I was a child, on the Eastern Shore of Maryland. I have very little remembrance of her, but I was inclined to believe she guided the pencil, as it was said she did, in Mary's hand. My wife and her uncle made a similar experiment with the same results.

A great many things occurred at my house for several months, which would require too much space. It was thus that my attention was first called to this subject.

The following written for, and published in the Memphis *Christian Advocate* in 1855, will show my views at that time.

MR. EDITOR—I have been solicited by several persons to write out my views upon spiritualism for the *Advocate*. Well, sir, I have found it a very difficult subject to understand. I have come to no satisfactory conclusion respecting it.

From the time the Rochester knockings commenced, to within a few months past, I have regarded it as the very "prince of humbugs." Although I read all I ever saw published upon the subject, I was not inclined to think it worthy of serious investigation; consequently I have never been at a regular circle—heard no lectures—seen no "*well-developed mediums*," though strongly urged to go and examine for myself, in New York and other places.

There is a class of persons whose bigotry is only equaled by their ignorance, (at least of this subject) who deny all well-authenticated facts in regard to it, and consider those who attach enough importance to the subject to investigate it, as having a "*weak point*," or "*going crazy*," or some other epithet of ridicule as being applicable to them. Such persons, to those who have investigated, only render themselves, more than the subject, ridiculous.

There is another class who have partially investigated, and have been satisfied there is some truth in it, yet are afraid of public opinion or something else, and so we often hear them say I do not want to know anything more about it.

I do not think, Sir, that I belong to either of these classes. I want to know its truth or falsity. If it is true that there is a medium through which we can converse with our departed friends, I want to know it. If it is false, and millions of our fellow-men are deceived in regard to it and led into dangerous error, it is the duty of every philanthropist to detect and expose the humbug. The only way, in may opinion, to accomplish this object, is to go into it thoroughly, probe to the bottom, and show its falsity in a *rational* and *consistent light*. As a Methodist preacher, it occurs to me that our ordination vows, to banish all erroneous and strange doctrines, would lead us to pursue this course in a frank, candid, and manly exposition of it.

I have been induced to make some investigation of this subject from manifestations which have been occurring at my house, and at others in this vicinity for some months past. It is not necessary to mention them in detail, but they have been somewhat similar to those which occurred in the Wesley family, for thirty-four years, mentioned by Dr. Clarke. Some, I know, will smile at what they think my delusion, and consider me humbugged too. Well, be it so—with such I have no argument at present. The phenomenon, whatever it is, has come to me—I have never gone in pursuit of it; I am satisfied that there is an influence brought to bear upon some persons who will, without any design upon their part, write *sensible, intelligent* answers to mental questions, which will astound the most skeptical. I have never said that I believed those communications were from the spirits of our departed friends, but I do say that all the laws of mind or matter with which I have ever become acquainted, utterly fail to explain to my satisfaction the *modus operandi* of these so-called spirit manifestations. I have seen a pencil placed n a pair of scissors, in the hand of a girl incapable of deception, and it would write answers to mental questions propounded; after which half a dozen persons would take the same pencil, placed in the same scissors, and with all their efforts could not make even a letter with it. To any unprejudiced mind this was ocular demonstration that there was power or influence controlling the pencil in her hand which we could not understand.

Infidelity, you know, has seized with avidity upon everything which would overthrow the divine authenticity of the Bible. Thus, many of the sciences have been thought to conflict with revelation, and shouts of triumph have been raised by skeptics; but subsequent investigations, however, have demonstrated that there is perfect harmony between science and revelation.

The fact is, if these communications are from spirits at all, many of them we know to be lying spirits. That there are lying spirits, no one who believes the Bible can doubt; for God himself sent a lying spirit to deceive Ahab. 1 Kings xxii. 20, 23.—God never designed to teach man in regard to the great principles of his moral government, and the relation he sustains to him, through such mediums; but by a revelation, marked with the "seal of high Divinity," demonstrated to be his infallible word by miracles of the most public character, and prophecies; hundreds of them, in regard to individuals, nations, kingdoms, and empires, which have been fulfilled in the world's history, and some of which are now being fulfilled.

All, therefore, who rely upon any such communications as these for light in regard to the future, and build their hopes of everlasting happiness upon what some "medium," perhaps himself of doubtful reputation, may say, will find he has built his house upon a sandy foundation, which will not stand in the judgment of the great day. My own opinion is that if these communications are from the spirit world, God has permitted them, to demonstrate to the materialist that there is a future state of existence after death. That there is a vast amount of infidelity in the world on this subject, no one who has paid any attention to the subject can doubt. Look at Europe, especially France and Germany, and we behold nations of infidels.

That we are upon the eve of the most important events the world has ever witnessed, I have no doubt. There have been famine, pestilence, and war. The mightiest nations of the earth are now being shaken, and God only knows what will be the result of these mighty convulsions. It becomes us, as watchmen on the walls of Zion, to keep a look out for the shadows which coming events cast before them. SAMUEL WATSON.

MEMPHIS, *August* 1, 1855.

A writer over the signature of "T." wrote to the editor of the *Advocate*, objecting to publishing my articles; after which I wrote the following:

BRO. COBB—I see by an editorial paragragh in the *Advocate* of the 15th Aug., that your friend "T." and others objected to your publishing my article upon Spiritualism a short time since. He certainly has a right to his opinion; so have others—some of whom, occupying the highest positions in Church and State, in this country, have approved of the article's being published in the *Advocate*, and have regretted the non-appearance of the other proposed. I can not see why a subject that is agitating the minds of so many, and making such high claims as Spiritualism does, " should be carefully excluded from the *Advocate ;*" especially, when those who believe in it are publishing so many ably edited newspapers and periodicals. The *Advocate and Journal*, *Nashville Advocate*, *New Orleans Advocate*, Northern *Methodist Quarterly Review*, and other religious papers, have all noticed it, and some of them have published a series of numbers in regard to it, admitting more than I ever believed to be true relative to the so-called spirit manifestations. At the solicitation of some friends whose opinions I felt bound to respect, I wrote what were my honest convictions respecting it; and while I admitted some facts which I could not explain by any principle of physics or metaphysics with which I was familiar, yet I was satisfied that no reliance was to be placed in them, and that those who consulted any such " *oracles*," to know any thing of their *spiritual and eternal interests*, were " led captive by the devil at his will;" that even to admit they were from spirits (which I have never done), they taught the doctrine of " ETERNAL DAMNATION " to the finally impenitent.

I shall not, however, wound the tender sensibilities of your friend " T." by writing any more for the *Advocate* on this subject.

I clip the following from the last number of the *Spiritual Telegraph*, purporting to come from a spirit of the highest authority in the spirit land:

" It is true that all who are **renewed by the spirit of**

God will progress and finally reach heaven, but those who do not yield their hearts to him will not progress—*they will sink to hell.*

"God assigns a place for all, and the place for the unrenewed of God's Holy Spirit is hell, below the seven spheres of which spirits speak. Except a man be born again, he can not see the kingdom of God. So said Christ on earth, and so he now says."

"There is no other name under heaven whereby men must be saved. Except ye be converted and become as little children, ye can not enter into the kingdom of God."

"The Bible is given to teach man what is necessary for him to know of his destiny, and how to make him happy, and whatever of spirit-teaching is contrary to the teaching of the Bible, is false."

The above has always been my opinion in regard to this subject; and as a Methodist preacher who has been in this conference ever since its organization, I felt inclined to give those views publicly. I had intended to have amplified more upon the subject, but will not trespass further upon your time and that of your patrons. If you see proper to publish this you are at liberty to do so; if not, it will make no difference.

I am, as ever, yours and the *Advocate's* friend,

SAMUEL WATSON.

MEMPHIS, *August* 28, 1855.

Thus ended my communications to the *Advocate* upon this subject. Though I was elected the next year by the Memphis Annual Conference to edit the same paper, and the year after elected by the General Conference, and continued its editor until 1866, yet I never wrote or published an article on that subject in it. The public mind was not prepared to examine it then, nor is it now, through that channel. St. Paul says: "If eating meat displease my brother, I will eat no more while the world standeth."

While thus perplexed in regard to these things—in the spring of 1855—a friend took the liberty to put my name with a select number to investigate the subject. There were five physicians, some of them now living in Memphis, now, as then, standing at the head of their profession. The different Churches of the city were represented by three ministers and several influential lay members. The head of the Episcopal Church in Tennessee was our leader. The medium was a native-born Memphian, an honest, pious young lady, a member of the Baptist Church.

With such persons I was willing to be associated to investigate the subject which was attracting so much attention. We always opened our meetings with prayer. We earnestly besought the Divine Spirit to direct us to the truth. Our meetings were religious, and produced a most hallowed influence on our minds and hearts. I cherish them now, though seventeen years have passed away, as the brightest spots in my history. If I have ever known what Bible Christianity was, it was greatly strengthened at those meetings. I preserved a considerable amount of manuscript, which I have copied as the main feature of the contents of what follows. If the reader believes we were deceived, he had as well close the book. We used every means in our power to prevent this, nor have I the least possible inducement to deceive others. I shall give what occurred, as best I can, from the documents and from memory, and leave all to receive or reject what they may see proper, from their stand, in regard to these things.

The first night was spent in the preliminaries of organization. The communications were made by the use of the alphabet. We were told that if we wished to investigate the subject, and would meet twice a week promptly, a spirit of olden time would meet with us and communicate with us. We were directed to open all our meetings with prayer precisely at the time appointed. After the organization there were physical manifestations such as we had never seen. At the request of any one, the large walnut extension-table would do anything that was asked, no one touching it but the medium, Miss Fisher. We could not question that all the laws, physical or metaphysical, with which we were acquainted could not explain what occurred without any visible agency. I made it a subject of special prayer for direction in what I had undertaken.

The next night Miss Fisher wrote, with great rapidity, answers to mental or oral questions that we propounded. We sat around the table, and would ask, in regular rotation, whatever we thought proper. There was a great diversity of interrogatories, upon various subjects, and answers, somewhat lengthy, written; showing very clearly that whatever controlled the pencil knew what was passing in the mind of the questioner. The spirit who had charge of us would not give us his name, nor the age or country in which he had lived. He wished to be known by the name of MYSTERY. He said he lived on earth several hundred years ago, and that Bishop Otey was familiar with his works. I must say I have never come in contact with a superior intelligence. Our meetings continued for several months, occupying usually about two hours each evening.

In all that he wrote, I do not remember anything that came in conflict with the general principles and doctrines as taught by the churches, with, perhaps, one exception. I must in candor say that he did state that in the intermediate state it was possible for those who had been wicked or undeveloped, if they would use the means there afforded, they might ultimately progress to a better state, but that there were many who lived in the early ages of the world still in outer darkness; that there, as well as here, persevering effort had to be made, in order to improve their condition. He taught us that PURITY OF HEART and life were essential to enjoy the society of the good; that we must have moral fitness before we could find a heaven anywhere. It was only the *pure*, the *good*, and the *holy* that could ever see or enjoy the kingdom of heaven; that there was a fearful hell—not of fire, but of remorse—for the wicked and the vicious, who thus passed into that state. The Church, he said, was the best place in which to prepare for the spiritual world; that they were not as pure as they should be, and that they took too materialistic a view of the Bible and the teachings of Christ; that there was a spiritual meaning to the Scriptures that many of them did not comprehend; that Christianity was a spiritual religion, and that the Bible, when properly understood, was the infallible guide to man He told us there were wicked, lying spirits, who were deceiving the people; that there were many of them in Memphis, and for us not to go among them. An editorial appeared in the *Eagle and Enquirer*, stating there was a circle that was taught that Christ was an impostor. Immediately after prayer, it was written, "Get the morning paper, and read what it says about me." He then appealed to us, in the most solemn manner, that we knew that was false, and that we owed it to truth, as well as to him, to contradict it through the same paper. We promised to do so, and the investigations continued as usual. At our next meeting, the first thing it asked was why we had not complied with our promise. I never saw a more severe castigation given for moral cowardice than he gave us. He told us he had left the high courts above, and important business, to come and teach us, and that we would suffer him to be slandered in the public prints, and. after promising, had failed to render him a simple act of justice, by stating what we knew to be the facts in the case. He told us that unless we did it over our own signatures he would never meet with us again. I remember distinctly his appeal to Bishop Otey. "You know," said he "what I have taught you all in regard to the divinity of Christ," quoting several of the strongest texts of Scripture relative to this doctrine. "I want you, Bishop, to write a separate card, stating the facts as they are, and the doctrines I have taught you." The card was drawn up, and we signed it. Bishop Otey wrote his, and they were published in the same paper, and form part of the history of those times. The bishop, editor, and most of those who signed the document, have passed over to the spirit land, where they see more clearly in regard to those things about which we were so intensely interested. Some of that number, however, remain on this side. They are now, as they were then, pious, intelligent, useful members of the different branches of the Church.

I propose to give some of the teachings of Mystery, and from other sources, corroborating the same general principles, leaving each one to exercise his own judgment as to the reliability of all that has been or may be written. I give it, not as my own, but merely as the teachings of what purported to have come from the spirit land.

We were often told to reject, as coming from lying, deceiving spirits, any and everything that was not in spirit sustained by the teachings of the Bible. With these cautions, I shall proceed, first, to notice what was said of the character of OUR LORD JESUS CHRIST. The *Supreme Being* assumed a human body, and arose, with its spiritual form, into heaven. He has become the *Divine* Man, and stands revealed in that humanity to the humble and loving children of his heavenly kingdom. This God, who is the Lord all in all of the heavens, is Jesus Christ. The Godhead, so far as it can be manifested to finite beings, exists in the divine humanity known historically to men of this earth as the Lord Jesus Christ. Said he not of himself,

"I am Alpha and Omega, the beginning and the end, which is, which was, and is to come" — the Almighty. A true conception of this subject will give a clear insight into some of the most remarkable things related in the Scriptures.

The same Divine Being has appeared to *patriarchs, prophets, apostles,* under many different forms; frequently as an angel called the "Angel of Jehovah," as a man wrestling all night with Jacob, as a man standing with a drawn sword before Joshua, as a man appearing to Abraham, as a human being dying a shameful death upon the cross, as a risen body showing to an unbelieving disciple the print of the nails and the mark of the spear, as a dazzling splendor on the Mount conversing with Moses and Elias, and as a form of light ascending to heaven. One of our number, Dr. Pittman, asked a great many questions in regard to the character of our Lord Jesus Christ. The answers were always in accordance with the Bible teachings respecting him; and the essential and eternal divinity was as clearly taught as I ever heard or read anywhere. Often the strongest texts of Scripture were quoted to establish the doctrine of the divinity of Christ. The first Epistle of John, 4th chapter, was particularly referred to, and the test there given of true and false spirits—the one confessing, the other denying this doctrine.

He said there was a diversity of opinion in the spiritual world, as well as here, in regard to the true character and mission of Christ; that those who were infidels here carried their opinions with them into the spiritual world, and entertained and propagated them until they were better informed; that what we call death does not change a man's character nor his opinions; and that we should not believe anything coming from that source any sooner than we would from any one here; but to try all by the infallible word of God, the BIBLE, as the only rock on which we should build our hopes for happiness when we pass from this into the other state of existence, to receive the full reward according to our works.

CHAPTER VII

GOD AND HEAVEN.

The representations which have been given of God by some who have been teachers of theology, have impressed the reflecting mind with erroneous ideas of his character. Whatever is truth, justice, and love in us, are the same in kind in us as in God; and it is absurd to think otherwise. The moral inadequacy of our thought of God is chiefly in this, that some have accepted as a teaching that he has a sovereign right to do what he likes with us, and that we have no business to judge as to the right or wrong of his actions. Some have taught that he creates to damn, or leaves us to ruin ourselves; or that he allows us to be children of the devil; things so absolutely immoral in an earthly father, that many men are driven into absolute revolt, or into a kind of hopeless, drifting carelessness of the whole matter.

These notions are unworthy of the God of the Bible, and they will all be done away with, by a true moral conception of God in his relations to us, based upon moral ideas which we ourselves possess of him. He has sent us forth from himself, therefore he is bound by the essential goodness of his nature, in the highest conceivable sense of a Father. Our aspirations are his voice in us. Our justice, truth, and love, such as they are, are still the same kind as his. He is a pure, moral being; therefore we must in the end be pure, moral beings, in order that we may enjoy that which is prepared for the pure in heart; as they alone shall ever enjoy God, which is eternal union with goodness, truth, and love. This, I think, will constitute the bliss of the heavenly state. "Be ye holy as I am holy," says God. "Be ye therefore perfect, even as your Father which is in heaven is perfect," says Jesus. These embody the essential elements of heaven. They constitute the necessary qualification for the enjoyment of heavenly employments. The threatenings as well as the promises of the Bible, are given as the motive power to stimulate all to seek that preparation of heart and life which alone will qualify them for the associations of the heavenly state. There is a profound philosophy in the religion of the Bible. If mankind were taught it properly, those who think correctly would see that the Gospel is not only "the power of God unto salvation," but that it is "the wisdom of God" to save all who have the requisite internal fitness of purity, without which no one can enjoy heaven.

It begins at the center, in a state of love and charity in the heart. That is the essential basis of its existence, the primal cause of its creation. No physical changes, no variations of place can bring a soul into heaven.

"The kingdom of heaven is within you," is the declaration of inspiration, and in perfect accord with the philosophy of religion. No learning, no wisdom, no spiritual illumination, no operations of the understanding can advance the spirit to the mansions of the blessed. Love to God in the heart, charity to the neighbor, obedience to the divine laws, a life according to the commandments— these are the passports to heaven, for these are the powers which create it, and animate and sustain it.

We shall understand more clearly what the occupations of these heavenly spirits are, if we first remove from our mind's eye everything calculated to obscure our perceptions of these earthly pursuits and earthly enjoyments which, by the very constitution of the spiritual world, are unnecessary or impossible in the future life.

The natural world is the sphere of birth and death. In the spiritual world nothing is born, nothing dies. The natural world is fixed in time and space; the spiritual world, where time and space are not realized as here.

In the natural world the occupations of life, with the feelings, ideas, motives, which they involve, are peculiar to the present state. They are necessary to this, our first stage of existence, and are the very means of our rational development, and of our preparation for a higher life. Their use, however, is only temporary, and they obscure our perception of spiritual things, and hide from us the riches and glory of our future inheritance. Our life here is a foregleam of immortality. This world is the seed field of elements which are to bear flower and fruit in heaven.

In our Father's house are many mansions, prepared for us by himself. We are to be fed with angels' food, a spontaneous creation, like the manna in the wilderness. The occupations of the other life are purely spiritual in their character. They all have reference to the growth and illumination of the mind, the purification of the affections, and to the sanctification of the will and the conduct of the life, on principles of love to the Lord and charity to the neighbor. To grow in wisdom, intelligence, goodness, and usefulness forever, is the life and felicity of heaven. The heavenly life is one of constant spiritual activity, in which every intellectual faculty of the mind, and every exalted affection of the heart, is called into blissful operation.

While I believe there is what may be called a local heaven, yet I think it will consist more in a state or condition than a place. The opinion that some people have of a material heaven seems to be absurd. They speak of it as a city, fifteen hundred miles square, with four gates on each side, with gold-paved streets, etc. They have God seated on a great white throne, and the people worshiping around it.

Such persons have taken the literal description given by St. John as their ideal, and think if they can only get through the gates they will be perfectly happy. Such persons have very erroneous ideas of God, we think, as well as of heaven. God is everywhere, filling immensity. It is a question whether we shall see God, only as he manifests himself through his Son, even in the spiritual world. It is time these early, childish notions of heaven were banished from the Church and the world—this dream-like state of existence, this quiescent mode of being, which would produce stagnation. We must have higher conceptions of the future life than those usually entertained, to restore to society a joyful belief in a blissful immortality. We want a picture of the world to come fitted to meet a larger and worthier ideal of the noble powers bestowed upon man.

God is represented as our Father. We are his children. The highest work of a father is the education of his children. The end of God's education of his creature, man, is the harmonious development of all his powers. All our faculties will have ample scope for expansion in the eternal world.

"I go to prepare a place for you," said our Saviour. A place for each one, fitted to his character, and to develop that character in perfection. In the doing of this, we shall have the continual delight of feeling that we are growing to the full expansion of all our powers. Our ideals shall become more beautiful, and minister continually to fresh aspirations, so that stagnation will be impossible. The outlines of life will be filled up, the rough statue of life shall be finished. We shall not only be spiritual men, but men complete in Christ. His intellectual nature will be more spiritual and refined when he becomes a "fellow-citizen with the saints;" and then all will be bound together by the omnipresent spirit of *love, goodness*, truth, and life, through Jesus Christ, our Saviour, "who redeemed us, not with corruptible things, as of gold, silver, or precious stones," but with his own peace-speaking blood, shed for every man.

Philosophy tells us that electricity can travel several hundred thousand miles in a second. If this be so who can conceive the velocity with which a pure spirit may pass through the universe of God. When we reflect upon the immensity of creation and the "infinity of space," we are lost in wonder, love, and praise, at the glorious prospective of man's destiny. While he may be in the full enjoyment of that "Eternal weight of Glory" in the upper sanctuary, his affinities may attract him to loved ones on earth, to impress the mind, and move the heart to virtue and happiness. These swift messengers of mercy who "minister to those who shall be heirs of salvation," have clear perceptions of the plan of human redemption. They know the intrinsic worth of the immortal spirit of man,— which is capable of such elevation. They know the priceless value of time, with all the privileges conferred by the gospel. They rejoice over the returning prodigal to his father's house, and the lost sheep that wandered from the fold. The minister of Christ may still be an "embassador for God," to bring about a reconciliation between the court of heaven and rebellious man. The work to which he consecrated his young heart and ripened manhood may be yet a part of his delightful employment, without the impediments that now attach to the work and office of the ministry. Not with railroad speed, but with angelic velocity will he travel in obedience to the will of his heavenly

Father. *Action,—vigorous, ceaseless activity*, is, I think, an essential requisite to happiness in that spiritual world. With an angel's ken we shall doubtless be permitted to look back upon our earth-history. Amid the revealing light of that world, every dispensation of the tangled web of human affairs will assume order and regularity, from the stand-point we shall then occupy. Then will be exhibited the most *perfect, beautiful symmetry* and harmony, where now we behold only discord and " confusion worse confounded." God's infinite *wisdom, love, power*, and goodness, were all employed in bringing us out of the mazy labyrinths through which we have passed in every part of our checkered history. Memory will revive every event of earth-life, and mark the goodness of God in those things over which we may have been disposed to murmur. We have seen the inscrutable acts of providence—our cherished plans have been frustrated, our dearest hopes have been disappointed, our brightest prospects have been blasted—our beloved ones have been taken away by the ruthless monster, while we have wept bitter tears of grief during days of weariness and sorrow—but blessed be God! there is a period fast approaching in our history when we shall see that these afflictions were blessings in disguise. We shall rejoice over those things, concerning which we have grieved. We shall see the goodness of God in transplanting the flowers to a more genial soil, to bloom on and bear fruit into everlasting life.

INTERMEDIATE STATE.

The world of spirits is a state of existence with its corresponding objective phenomena, into which all men are ushered immediatly after death. This state is that which exists between heaven and hell. This is the Sheol of the Old Testament, the Hades of the New, erroreously translated in our English Bible as hell, and the grave. Josephus expressly defines the word Sheol, which our translators render hell, as "the place wherein the souls of the righteous and the unrighteous are detained." It was universally accepted as an article of rational faith in the Christian Church until the time of Luther.

When death performs its office, we pass into this state, the same that we were in in the present state of being. The material body returns to the earth, while the spiritual body, with all its mental and moral identity, passes into this state. The mere act of death produces no change in the affections, thoughts, opinions, or aspirations of man. The laws of the spiritual world instantaneously operate upon him. He comes into the exercise of spiritual thought. He speaks, spontaneously, the rich and wonderful language of spirits. He cannot enter heaven, because his spiritual state of affection and thought are not in accord with those of the angels. He could neither see nor hear what they saw and heard. It is not possible for any one to enter that heavenly society without a fitness for their association. He would tremble at his evil thoughts and desires. His life would project itself outwardly around them in terrible, disgusting forms. Such a thing is organically impossible. It is plain that the law of spiritual relation demands and effects the total separation of the good and evil, so that heaven and hell stand eternally apart.

The world of spirits is, to outward appearance, a vast world, not fixed in time and space, like our natural world, but plastic and changeable to the outflowing thoughts and affections of its inhabitants. It appears differently, to different classes of spirits who live there. The form this world assumes to those who recently deceased is very much like that of the world they have left. The reason is this: They are still in possession of their exterior *memory, thoughts, affections,* and *life,* for man has an external and an internal life. His exterior life has been taken away from him. His interior nature has come out to view. They no longer have two faces. They no longer think one thing and say another. All external bonds and restraints are removed, forgotten, despised. There is no fear of the law or public opinion; no influence of fashion, no respect for wealth or position, no sacrifices to decorum, no concealment from interested motives. The man or the woman stands out in utter spiritual nakedness—every thought, every feeling exposed to view. Outward organizations are now nothing. Conventionalisms perish; their own names and history are shadows. Their qualities alone survive. From them they think, see, live. Here is the separation of good and evil spirits, and the separation of good and evil elements in the individual spirit. No evil passions, no false opinions, no unruly tempers, no frailties cleave to the good man.

Not only are the dead of whole generations there, but angels from heaven and evil spirits are there. Our attendant spirits are there; our guardian spirits, who befriend and guide us, are there; and the evil spirits who tempt us are there. Searching are the methods, inexorable the processes, and fearful the revelations of the world of spirits. Double dealing is detected, the hypocrite unmasked and exposed, and the soul without the wedding garment is cast out from the feast into "outer darkness."

On the other hand, the good are delivered from temptation and trial, restored to spiritual sight and hearing; relieved, strengthened, comforted, and purified. All this is done without infringing upon the free agency of any spirit, without any compulsion or violence.

These wonderful operations going on in the spiritual world are of immense importance to us. They are not far off, like the historical events of some distant planet, they are immediately over and around us; yea, are within us. We are nearing the heaven or hell to which we are going. "We can not serve two masters." We must choose between them. We are now serving the one or the other, and thus making the place we shall have assigned us. We have the elements of a heaven or a hell forming within us in the present state of being. How precious, then, is time, with all its privileges. Its importance can not be properly estimated until we shall see things in their true light. Then we will see that that is the substance, this the shadow; that the waking day, this the dream of night. One has faded away, the other is to live forever. O, if we could realize these truths, how different would mankind act in the present infant state of our being!

SPIRIT COMMUNION.

There are vast numbers of persons through whom spirits can communicate, either by *mental* or *physical manifestations*. This is not done by a miracle or special providence, nor by the suspension of God's immutable laws, but it has been in accordance with and in execution of these laws. There may be spirits too gross to approach up to a level of your stage of existence, but, with that exception, all the spirit world, whether wise or foolish, vicious and evil-disposed, or virtuous and holy, can alike exercise the prerogative of communing.

Many spirits, bound to the earth by the strong ties of attachment for those whom they have recently left, are anxious to commune with them. Many who have too long ago passed away to have any such personal ties, are still drawn to earth by the propensities which have marked their life here, and which still linger around them. Some wish to commune from an unselfish desire to alleviate the condition of mankind; others, alas! feeling the passions which tainted their mortal career, desire to commune in gratification of their peculiar disposition while they lived on earth. As the reality of spirit intercourse was the natural law of man's progression, all the various classes of spirits could commune, the one as well as the other. This accounts for, and explains that conflict of opinion which exists in the spiritual as in the natural world.

One great idea belonging to death has scarcely been apprehended or appreciated. Death is the continuance of life. It is life without the restraints imposed upon it by the limits of a single planet. Now, though it is important that the designs of life should be investigated and understood, it certainly is of as much importance that that life, in its continuance, should be perfectly appreciated. The one is of short duration, the other is for eternity. This, then, is the object of spirit communion; and it behooves all to understand what they believe, that they may, when satisfied themselves, be able to satisfy others.

The angels who are not men, mentioned in the Bible, I am led to believe were once men, whose organization has passed the last process of refinement, and are constantly with all that can be known of God.

No human mind, however fertile in imagination, can picture, in its wildest fancy, the overpowering and transcendent beauty of the progressed and elevated soul. The world's images of thought fail to convey the faintest idea of my meaning. Those beings once passed through a similar process of development, by having a material body, in some other world. God is uniform and unchangeable in his laws and principles. He thus reveals himself to us in the Bible, without which we could know nothing of such a being. His laws are uniform—adapted to all worlds, and to all created intelligences which he has brought into existence by his Almighty power. When the plans and purposes of God shall have been effected, and earth be redeemed from the thraldom of sin, by the Gospel, then the final triumphant destiny that awaits the redeemed shall be accomplished. Then, all that is necessary to constitute the essential elements of our personal individuality shall come forth, like unto "our Saviour's glorious body," and "meet him in the air, and ever be with the Lord." Then shall the Church triumphant enter upon the glorious fruition of the "eternal weight of glory" reserved in heaven for the pure and the good of every age and nation.

CHAPTER VIII.

THE SPIRITUAL WORLD.

This is a world, composed of all the forms necessary to constitute a real world. It is as distinct, substantial, and real, to those who have entered it, as this world is to those who live here. Most persons think of it as above them, somewhere in the realms of space. Where is it? From all I have been able to learn of it, from the Bible, it is very near us. It is not spoken of as far away in the center of the universe (as Dr. Dick supposes) but around, and within the material universe. We are now in this world, though we may not be conscious of it. Why then, it may be asked, can we not see it? I answer: some of the most powerful agents in nature can be seen only by the effects they produce. Many instances are given in the Bible of persons who saw it, while they were still in this world. They are spoken of as having their "eyes opened," or "being in the spirit." The spiritual eye is veiled by the material. Its organization is too delicate to be acted on by the gross forms of matter. Our spiritual senses are ordinarily asleep, and we cannot see the spiritual world about us until they are awaked. None but the materialist believes that the natural body is the man. It is only the house in which he lives. Where is the spirit world? This is a question more easily asked than answered. I believe that it surrounds, and permeates the natural world. What stupendous interests revolve around the replies to this question? What light their truthful answers would cast upon the great mysteries of life and death? How singularly averse is the popular mind, under the tuition of the passing dispensation, to think of the spiritual world as a real, and substantial state of existence. The Bible itself is in a measure a dead letter in the eyes of a sensual and philosophizing generation. The very people who believe it, and love it, and preach it, cannot realize that the Bible shows us that angels, and departed spirits are living already in the human form, seeing, feeling, and loving as we do. Each soul is responsible for its heaven, or its hell. We make the one, or the other according to the intellectual and moral status of each individual, who determines by its state or condition where, and with whom, and how, it shall live forever. No arbitrary or judicial decree lifts it to heaven, or dooms it to hell. The same law which raises the *pure* and the *holy* to heaven, sinks the *wicked* and the *vicious* to hell. There must be qualification before there can be enjoyment, even in heaven. There must be the kingdom of heaven within the soul, before it can ever find a heaven in the universe of God. This is sound philosophy, as well as the plain teachings of the Bible. Our life and conduct on earth, will fix and determine our external surroundings to all eternity. We are every day contributing something to make up the character which we shall carry with us into the other life. Death, as we call the separation of the natural from the spiritual body, will not, can not produce any change in the intellectual, or moral character of the individual.

Man is an epitome of the universe. We can conceive of nothing that is not material or spiritual; so that in him are blended these two principles of which the universe is composed. We have rational *natural, spiritual, celestial* degrees of being folded away in potency behind, and within the flesh and blood of this life. They are gradually opened, by instruction, discipline, and experience, by the developement of the rational principle, by temptations, by a life according to the commandments, by a reception of love and wisdom from the Lord, who giveth to all, liberally, talents to improve, work to perform in proportion to the capacity given. And in the exact ratio of our improvement of what has been bestowed upon us will be the capacity which we shall have for the enjoyment of that which awaits us in the future state. *God is good;* "His tender mercies are over all his works," and he will fully justify his ways to man. "I am the God of Abraham, the God of Isaac, and the God of Jacob." "He is not the God of the dead, but of the living." If there is any force in this reasoning, Abraham, Isaac, and Jacob are still living, as real, substantial beings. They preserve there personality, and identity. Moses and Elias, who appeared at the transfiguration, are still living as distinct human beings. Lazarus and the rich man recognize each other. The patriarchs and prophets constitute a part of that "cloud of witnesses" of whom St. Paul says "they were stoned and sawn asunder." Death is the withdrawal of the man himself from the body, and by this act steps into the spiritual world himself. We see the material features, colors, motions, changes; but we do not see the real human being. That dwells within, and can only manifest itself through the veil of the body. All that you see is the material covering of the spiritual being.

We can not demonstrate the spiritual world and the spiritual body to the natural senses. We can not see and feel, with the natural senses, a spiritual form, ordinarily. St. Paul calls the one the "outward man," the other the "inward man." One is of the "earth, earthy," the other the breath of the Almighty. The Bible regards the "inner man," the spirit, as the real man. Its whole scope, form, and purpose are directed to man as a spiritual being. His body is then spiritual, and, thus separated from earthly things, touches and sees that which is spiritual, just as when what is natural touches and sees what is natural. In a word, when a man passes from one life into the other, or from one world into another, he carries with him his *intellectual, moral, spiritual* identity. This change does not affect his moral status—what we call death has no power to change the character of any one. He also carries with him his natural memory. "Son, remember," said Abraham to the rich man. It is a very common idea that the spiritual state is vague, indistinct, *shadowy, unreal;* but this is directly the reverse of the truth. This world is the shadow, that is the substance. That is far more real and distinct to every sense. Every person becomes more individualized. All are seen in their real character—there are no hypocrites there. The more holy we have been here, the happier we will be there. There are no assignable limits that the regenerate soul must not pass. What shall we become when millions of years shall have passed away? *Onward, upward,* forever rising, forever perfecting, forever nearer the Lord. "It doth not yet appear what we shall be." The highest angel may not conceive it. Oh, the grandeur, the glory, the blessedness of the human destiny to all eternity!

One of the most important and deeply interesting questions that can engage the attention of man is, Where are the dead? The materialist believes that the soul, or mind, dies with the body, and that the grave closes the history of man. There are others, who claim to take the Bible for their authority, who believe that the intervening time between death and the resurrection is, or appears to be, but a moment. Hence they have been called "soul-sleepers." From each of these we differ as widely as the mind of man can well conceive, as will appear by the following views which we entertain. It will thus be seen that it is an unsettled question with the great body of mankind, where those who have passed away from earth have gone, and with many whether they have any existence. With us it is not a question to be settled as to their existence. We have sufficient evidence to make it a matter of knowledge, at least so far as their existence is concerned. If, however, the where, as to place or locality, perhaps we can not say with certainty of knowledge. The two worlds can not be very far apart, as Stephen, the first martyr, saw, even while they were stoning him to death, into heaven, and the glorified body of Jesus. The question we raise here is, Where are the friends who depart from our sight here, leaving their earthly bodies to molder to their mother earth? Are they still in conscious, personal identity, and with us, at least occasionally, to minister to us? Nearly all the writers and speakers who refer to the dead, to spirits and spirit life, treat the subject morally, socially, and intellectually, and present many wild, and some rational theories of spirit life; but there is a vagueness in regard to the whereabouts of the spirit world which has always prevailed in the Christian teachings. They have a heaven and a hell, but they are not located anywhere. All must admit that condition constitutes a part of what constitutes the one and the other. We often hear of time and space being annihilated. This may be true in regard to some of God's creatures, but those who are in the "intermediate state" must know something of them. To us it seems not only Scriptural but quite reasonable, that spirits who have lived and loved on earth, who have many and strong attachments, would have strong attractions to persons and places left behind; and it seems equally reasonable to us that at some distant day with some, and at no very distant day with others, they will loose the binding attractions of earth, and hold no further intercourse with its inhabitants. The belief in a future state, especially among educated people, is not so universal as many suppose. There is much infidelity in the world, and some in the Church, on this subject. We have often heard some of the best Christians express their doubts and fears in class and love-feast meetings. I rejoice to know that there is a stand-point from which we may look, not only by faith in the reality of spirit existence and intercourse with mortals, but realize, beyond the possibility of doubt, that they are cognizant of our events, and are interested in us still. These are vital questions to the soul, yet many teachers of religion step over them like a school-boy going through a grave-yard, and rejoice when they reach the farther side. Being afraid of appearing wise above what is written, they ignore what is written. The revelations of the Bible are few. It was certainly not given to gratify even what we may consider a laudable curiosity. The light is only scattered rays. The sparseness of the revelations deter people from researches in that direction. The Scriptural arguments are twofold: 1, Inferential; 2, Direct. The Scriptures teach that we are living in close contact with the spirit world; that the inhabitants of that world are in our midst, and that it only needs the eye of the soul to be opened for us to see

> "Angels now are hov'ring round us,
> Unperceived amid the throng."

The Bible teaches us that thousands of beings are deeply interested in the affairs of this earth. The earth was their birthplace, the scene of their conflicts and triumphs. It is the residence of their relatives and friends.

> "Can a mother's tender care
> Cease toward the child she bare?"

Never, no, never! If she is the same being she was while

she was endeared to them while here, she would rather lead the anthem of the heavenly choir. Can they, when they cross the line, or pass the veil which divides the spiritual from the natural world, lose the interest they have in loved ones left behind? The departed good take great interest in the career of the Christian. If angels rejoice over the conversion of a sinner, shall not the sainted mother, who has thousands of times prayed for her gay daughter or profligate son, rejoice over their conversion? Oh, if we could open the eyes of our "inner" man, and see as the prophet's servant did when, in answer to his prayer, the veil was withdrawn, we would see an "innumerable" host of God's messengers around us, ready to aid us in the conflicts of life. Among them we would, doubtless, recognize many familiar faces of loved ones, for whom we have shed many bitter tears of sorrow because of our separation. They have passed through similar trials, and are prepared to sympathize with those who remain in the present state. Says the apostle, "Ye are come unto Mount Zion, and unto the City of the living God, the heavenly Jerusalem, and to an innumerable company of angels, to the general assembly and church of the firstborn, which are written in heaven, and to God, the judge of all, and to the spirits of just men made perfect." Joseph Benson, in his commentary on this passage, says, "The spirits of saints in paradise, with whom the saints on earth have communion by faith, hope, and love, and make up one body with them." "Hence it is evident," says Whitty, "that the souls of just men are not reduced by death to a state of insensibility; for can a soul that reasons and perceives good things, be made perfect by perceiving nothing at all?"

We shall continue to live on after our bodies molder away to dust. Our souls shall live in a state of consciousness, and be happy or miserable, as our lives on earth have been pure and good, or vicious and evil. How important, then, to be "pure in heart, for they shall see God," and be his ministering angels to those who shall be heirs of salvation.

This spiritual world I believe surrounds and permeates the natural world; that it is as real and, to spirits, as tangible as the natural world.

Into this world the spirits of the departed go after what we call death passes over them. It is the place to which the Saviour went between his crucifixion and his resurrection. Hence he said to the penitent thief who prayed to him on the cross, "This day shalt thou be with me in paradise." After his resurrection, he said to Mary, "Touch me not, for I am not yet ascended to my Father; but go to my brethren, and say unto them I ascend to my Father and your Father, and to my God and to your God." Forty days subsequent to this he did ascend to his Father, as recorded in Acts i. 9, 10: "And when he had spoken these things, while they beheld, he was taken up, and a cloud received him out of their sight. And while they looked steadfastly toward heaven, as he went up, behold two men stood by them in white apparel; which also said, 'Ye men of Gallilee, *why* stand ye gazing up into heaven? This same Jesus, which is taken up from you into heaven, shall so come in like manner as ye have seen him go up into heaven.'"

St. Stephen, the first who sealed the truth of his religion with his own blood, "being full of the Holy Ghost, looked up steadfastly into heaven, and saw the glory of God, and Jesus standing at the right hand of God; and said, 'Behold, I see the heavens opened, and the Son of Man standing on the right hand of God.'" His spiritual vision was opened, as multiplied thousands have been since, even before the spirit left the body, to see the glories of the eternal world.

We have seen the Saviour of the world pass through this intermediate state, burst the bands of death asunder, and ascend on high, where he ever liveth, as our great High-Priest, to make intercession for us. But the question is, Will the saints pass, directly after death, into this upper sanctuary of the Most High? I think not. They are not prepared for it. Death will give them no qualification for it. John Wesley says: "It is very generally supposed that the souls of good men, as soon as they are discharged from the body, go directly to heaven; but this opinion has not the least foundation in the oracles of God." Bishop McTyeire commences a sermon in the *Methodist Pulpit, South* by saying: "No one has ever yet been saved in heaven, no one sent to hell."

Where, then, do they go? is the question. What are their employments during their stay in that intermediate state? I think we may learn somethtng in regard to them by referring again to our Saviour. St. Peter tells us (1 Peter, iii. 18): "For Christ hath once suffered for sins, the just for the unjust, that he might bring us to God, being put to death in the flesh, but quickened by the Spirit. By which also he went and preached unto the spirits in prison, which sometimes were disobedient." "Prison" here, we are told, should have been translated "spirit world" or "paradise."

There are some who believe that this place of departed spirits is away off in some planet, where they are resting from their labors, in a kind of quiescent state, waiting for the resurrection of the body, and that all the knowledge they have of what is transpiring on earth is derived from those who have left it since they sojourned below; that messages may be sent to those who are there by those who pass on, but they can receive no message from them in return.

I think that those who entertain such opinions have not

a correct idea of the Bible-teaching on that subject. They are represented as taking a deep interest in the affairs of this world, ministering to those whom they love, and doing all they can, consistently with the free agency of man, to help him to "work out his own salvation." As Christ preached, during his stay there, to the inhabitants of that country, so our loved ones will have charge of us, and "encamp around us," while we remain in the Church militant. The best evidence we can have on this subject is the express declaration of our Lord Jesus Christ. He said to Nicodemus—though patriarchs and prophets, with countless millions of earth's inhabitants, had, during the four thousand previous years of the world's history, died—"If I have told you earthly things, and ye believe not, how shall ye believe if I tell you of heavenly things? And no man hath ascended up to heaven but he that came down from heaven, even the Son of Man, which is in heaven." John iii. 12, 13. This, it seems to me, would forever settle this question with those who believe in the supreme knowledge of Him who alone "came down from heaven" to redeem us.

St. Paul (Hebrews xi.), after enumerating the host of pious men and women, from Abel down, of whom "the world was not worthy," says, "These all having obtained a good report, through faith, received not the promise, God having provided some better thing for us, that they, without us, should not be made perfect." I think it probable that the pious and good of every age and nation may enter the supernal heavens together; but as to their state between the death of the body and this glorious coronation of the saints, I think they are actively engaged in the great work of "ministering to those who shall be heirs of salvation." It will constitute their employment, and be the most conducive to their enjoyment.

I shall never forget the sermon preached by the Rev.

Dr. Winans, in the city of New Orleans, over thirty years since. It was the funeral of Rev. Elijah Steel, who sacrificed his life visiting the sick and dying of yellow fever there. Said the immortal Winans "Elijah Steel did much in this city for the sick and dying by pointing them to Christ, but he has entered upon a much larger field of usefulness. He can now, with the rapidity of thought, go, as a pure ministering spirit, to the same great work in which he sacrificed his life. Whenever God has more use for his servants in the spiritual world, than he has here, he takes them to labor in the same glorious cause, with greatly enhanced facilities, doing his will on earth as it is done in heaven."

I was sojourning in the sunny clime expecting to fall a victim to that scourge of the human race—consumption. This view of that subject removed the last difficulty in my way of dying. If that is to be my mission still, let me pass over the river, and enter upon it, I thought, as the preacher spoke of the glorious privilege confered upon the servants of Christ to be as the angels—messengers of God to minister to loved ones on earth. This has afforded me more comfort than anything, from that time to the present; more especially, since I have had such demonstrations in regard to it, corroborated by the declarations of God's inspired word. We can, not only send messages to them by those who go "over there," but we can have messages direct from them, of the most consolatory character, cheering us on to the performance of the various duties we owe to others in this state, as the order of Providence opens for doing good to all, thus working out a destiny here, preparatory for that which awaits us in the "other life," so near the present state of existence. Oh, if we could only see with our spirit eyes now, we should behold an "innumerable company of angels . . . and the spirits of the just men made perfect" constituting the heavenly host of God, to aid the sons and daughters of men to come off victorious in all the spiritual conflicts of life, and finally to triumph over the last enemy. And when they pass out of the material and enter upon the spiritual to welcome them to enter upon the delightful employment of doing for others what has been done for them through their earthly pilgrimage. Then shall we rejoice over the returning prodigal to his father's house, and the lost sheep that wandered from the fold. We shall continue to love our friends on earth, and, as our affinities must attract us to them while they remain here, it will be our delight to do whatever we may be permitted, consistently with their moral agency.

The facilities or spiritual elevation will be similar there to what they have been here. In proportion as we help others, in that ratio will be developed our capacity for enjoyment. As the atmosphere contains electricity, by which we can communicate with each other, all around the world, so we believe the spiritual world will be to all pure spirits without any of the physical machinery necessary here. As our natural body telegraphs its members and we carry with us a mental atmosphere, by which mind impresses mind, so we believe in paradise all those who are in affinity will hold sweet communion, without the use of language as a vehicle of thought through which to express our ideas—spirit can hold intercourse with spirit by intuition. Oh, what wonderful capacity is possessed by this master-work of God, in the endless development of the faculties with which man is endowed, and the vast theater upon which he is destined to act, ever approximating perfection.

CHAPTER IX.

KNOWLEDGE OF SPIRITS.

WE once asked Mystery if the spirits could tell of future events. His reply was, "They can not. They can, however, occupying, as they do, a much more elevated stand-point than mortals, with the power to see the operations of the minds of human beings in and out of the material body, form a much more correct opinion as to the effect of causes not seen by them." He told us emphatically that no human intelligence could know with certainty the future. None but the Infinite God, who comprehends time and eternity, could see what was in the future. Corresponding with this, I find the following in Judge Edmund's and Dr. Dexter's work, as coming from the spirit of Bacon:

"We do not pretend to prescience, but we do avow our power to combine all the workings of mind and matter, which we behold under different and more favorable circumstances than yourself, and bring the influence to bear on the present or future condition of the one for whom the observations were made. We are no fortune-tellers, but we read events only by comparison; and thus, those of your friends who love you, and who, when on earth, were active and prominent in the busy scenes of life, have specially collated the opinions and feelings of your professed friends, and, reading their very hearts, understand, therefore, what would be their probable action.

"Spirits differ but little from men, except in the sublimation of their organism and in the stronger exercise of the attributes of their minds. Thus, their judgment on matters connected with their life is more matured, and the grand characteristics of their minds are more developed. Their feelings and desires are more intense than man's, and they aspire higher than man, for they are not satisfied with the pleasures and joys of their state, but are continually striving to enter higher in the scale of intellectual and moral happiness.

"PROGRESSION, ONWARD, UPWARD, FOREVER! New scenes, new countries, new stages of progress, one above another, without end. They come to earth, to beseech mortals no longer to grovel in the earth, seeking their enjoyment in earthly objects, but to look up, up, and from on high shall come to them the knowledge that shall make them free. They teach them that *happiness* and *heaven* do not come to them as a gratuity, but that they must labor and toil for that which is good and pure. They teach them that God does not work by miracles, but by eternal, immutable laws, which are all powerful to save, almighty to condemn, and which are not found in the glasses of men, but are written by his Almighty hand."

I shall avail myself of some extracts from communications written by Judge Edmunds for the New York *Tribune* on this subject.

"Led by the education and religious teaching which we have, both in youth and in manhood, from the pulpit as well as in school, we are apt to attach to the idea of spirit existence that of great, if not omniscient, knowledge; and if we imbibe the belief that spirits speak to us, we naturally expect from them the display of knowledge far superior to ours. This is a great error, for we pass into the spirit world just as we are here, in respect to knowledge, and have no more than we had here until we learn it. When, therefore, a spirit speaks to us, it is not with omniscience, but with such knowledge only as he has been able to acquire. There is, therefore, infinite variety, in this respect, among spirits depending upon education while on earth, opportunities for learning in the spirit world, intellectual capacity, and many other things, which there, as well as here, affect the training of the mind. So far as spirits speak of their existence or mode of life there, each must naturally know only of what he has observed, unless, perchance, he has been taught more by others, who have beheld what he has not. At all events, most of the incongruous teachings referred to are in reference to what spirits have beheld. Now there, as well as here, no two behold precisely the same thing. Each views the scene around each, and there must, therefore, of necessity, be the same discrepancies which we behold here when we are taking human testimony respecting human events, or even inanimate scenery. Each beholds from a different stand-point from the other, and there must, therefore, be different accounts.

"So, too, there is a great difference in the power of observation and the faculty of expression. We behold around us here men who can see nothing clearly; others, again, who see clearly, but have a bungling and obscure mode of expressing themselves. These peculiarities accompany the spirit into his spirit life, and must mark his intercourse with us until he shall have so far advanced as to have eradicated those defects. But until he shall so advance, it will be in vain to expect from him communications marked by clearness of perception and expression, which we are so fain to suppose ought to characterize all spiritual intercourse. The very fact of its absence tends to show us the great truth, what the change is which death works in us, namely, that though we leave our physical nature behind, intellectually and morally we are the same, and the spirit is but the continuation of mortal life; that the real, or inner man, is the same, with all his improvements and perversions, just as they were when he laid aside his outer garment, but with the advantage of greater means of obtaining knowledge, and less obstacles to its acquisition. There is another difficulty, for which the spirit world is not responsible, and that is, that the mind of the medium does, and must, more or less affect the communications.

"Occasionally there are instances where it would seem as if the medium were giving the precise words of the spirit; but this is rare, because it involves a state of things in the medium, both physically and mentally, that is very difficult to attain, namely, an exclusion of the medium's selfhood—a suspension of his own will and spirit control—that is very unnatural, very difficult and dangerous, and, therefore, necessarily very rare. The most favored instances of this character which I have witnessed are those where the medium speaks a language unknown to him, and he all the time, though conscious he is speaking, is unconscious what idea he is conveying. It is to the medium as if he were uttering unmeaning gibberish.

"He does not see by the physical light which we use, neither by the light of our sun, nor our lamps nor our fires. Each, as I understand it, engenders his own light, which is greater or less according to his condition, morally and intellectually; and they are frequently aided by each other's light. But how much this enables them to behold of the mortal or spiritual life which surrounds them it is difficult to say. This, however, I have discovered, that there are things immediately around and before them, in both states of existence, which they do not behold, and of whose presence they are entirely unconscious. For instance, Bacon, who has been nearly three hundred years in the spirit world, with all his intellectual powers and culture, has been, while communing with me, ignorant that another spirit was at the same time doing so, and ignorant even that this spirit was present. One of my brother judges, shortly after his death, came to me, and in his communion with me was ignorant of the presence of another spirit who stood by his side, and who was as visible to me as he was, and, without entering too much into detail, I will remark that I have had very many evidences of this.

"Man's condition in the spirit world, as I am taught, depends on his progress in Purity, in Love, and Knowledge. It is progress in purity which fixes the plane on which he exists there, while it is his progress in knowledge and love which controls his associations on this plane."

CONFESSION TO EACH OTHER.

One of the most solemn meetings we ever had, occurred near the close of our investigations. Mystery told us that we must, each of us, one by one, tell to the others what were our besetting sins—"not as the ignorant Romanist makes his confession to the priest, but, as the apostle says, confess your faults one to another, and pray one for another." We knew that he saw the working of our minds, and we began at the head and went round. Each one told what he thought was his worst trait of character. It was, indeed, a trying time to some of the circle; yet I believe each of us made confession as in the presence of God and angels, whom we were assured were present. He told us that he would be a Judas, if any one spoke to others of what we had confessed to each other that night.

"I have never," he said, "in my intercourse with you, flattered the selfish propensities of your nature. They, of themselves, are all-powerful; and they usurp the mind when least suspected. They maintain possession, sometimes, under the garb of an earnest desire for independent thought and action; but when to the soul the true character of these feelings are laid open, how fearfully it has been deceived! My friends, the life given you is one filled with all manner of temptation besetting you on every side, and so varied and multifarious, that you are deceived ere you are aware that you have been tempted. Could we meet you face to face, and impress on your senses the undoubted evidence of our identity, you might recognize that you were indeed destined to live with us forever, or to dwell in those dark spheres below us, where the light of truth is scarcely manifest. The thoughts that agitate your souls and excite the action of your selfish propensities, must be laid under the stern control of your pure desire to love nothing, to know nothing, and to live for nothing but the truth as it is from God.

" That your hearts, pure and undefiled, may meet the response of those of your friends; that you may indeed bear each other's burdens, and assist each other in your pilgrimage toward and through the spheres, I greet you in the fullness of undying love, and I charge you to open your thoughts to one another, and to mingle your affections and aspirations together, that together you may wander toward the mark of your high calling, which is the development of your natures. It is well that your own hearts are brought up before the bar of strict examination, and all the passions and feelings which have governed them are exposed to the searching investigation of truth."

CHILDREN AFTER THEIR DEPARTURE.

It is a question of deep interest to parents who have been called to mourn over their separation from their loved ones—Will they remain children, or will they grow up to maturity in that intermediate state into which they enter when they leave earth? Having had nine thus pass away I have felt a great anxiety to know, if possible, what would be their ultimate condition. It is clear to my mind that children grow in the other life to the full stature they would have attained had their material bodies matured in this world. Shall I find my children in that better land, and will they know me? Do they know me now?

Do these sweet little beings hover about me? I believe they can, and do visit us. They are not immersed in the great ocean of human existence. My boys are mine still. My sweet little daughters will ever be mine. In my heart, I feel they will ever be my children. Heaven would not be complete without them. There will be lines and lineaments by which I shall identify them without the clogs of this mortal life. Such love cannot be quenched with everlasting forgetfulness. No, never! Heaven is real! Love is eternal! Family ties, severed here, will be reunited forever. They are not lost to us, only separated for a while by the veil between us. O glorious, blessed truth revealed, of meeting over the river, to separate no more forever!

They would be imperfect without that growth which is necessary for them to attain the object of their being. Their spirits grow, and expand, and assume very much the character they would have had if they had lived and matured here. Children are taught by pure spirits, and soon become capable of appreciating some of the laws of God which affects their nature, and as their ideas are not mixed, or amalgamated with the crudities of animal organization, they are more clear and comprehensive than even some spirits who have been in the spirit land for years.

"Little children have often special missions confided to them, and are often sent to earth to perform offices and duties of a high character. Spirits are not judged by age, but by purity. It is a law there, and it is certain evidence of ability, for a spirit who loves God without guile can also understand the laws which bind man to man, and those also which God has established for the government of the same.

"Little children are often selected to accompany their parents during their stay on earth, and the mother is often surrounded by developed spirits, even of those whose birth she had not numbered with those living or dead. In the dark hour of trial, when the widowed mother is struggling with poverty to support and educate the living ones, then it is that the spirits of their children are sent to earth clothed with dazzling beauty and gifted with powers to soothe and calm the troubled spirit of that mother. Gently, and yet serenely instilling hope, where before all was dark despair, and raising the drooping heart with confidence and trust to God, who is a husband to the widow and a father to the orphan. Children though they may have grown in the spirit world can appear when they desire to do so, as they did when they passed away from earth. Spirits have the power to appear and usually do appear as they did when on earth."

Thus when Samuel appeared he was described by the woman to Saul as 'an old man coverd with a mantle.' For more than two years his body had been deposited in the earth, yet he appears to the man whom he had anointed as the first king of Israel just as Saul had seen him during his natural life. This is as clear as any other fact recorded in sacred history, and establishes an important principle—Gods laws are unchangeable, like himself.

Truth and principle are eternal. Whatever has been done in any age may, under the same circumstances, be done in any other. If persons who lived on earth did return and converse with mortals under the *patriarchal*, the *Mosaic*, and the prophetic *dispensation*, shall such manifestations be withheld under the Christian dispensation? There is nothing that we find anywhere in the Bible or the laws of God to justify a denial of such manifestations—Dr. Bond's opinion to the contrary notwithstanding.

The infant mind will not have that slow, vegetative process of acquiring knowledge that it has here. That it will, like all other intelligences, begin there with what it gained here is, I think, certain. They will have faculties far surpassing those enjoyed in this state of existence. There has been such close union between the soul and the body, that the former has sympathized with the latter, which has clogged its aspirations. Now it breathes a heavenly atmosphere, and engages in angelic employments. What are these? is a question of deepest interest to those who think of a life which is to come. We may not be able to comprehend here how a departed spirit can see, hear, know, and converse; yet there is light that shines upon the subject from the Scriptures and the philosophy of our spiritual natures, which gives us clear conceptions of what shall be a part of our employment in the intermediate state. Who that has ever thought of the nature of man, that does not know that he was made for action? Even in the garden of Eden employment was given him, in order to happiness. It is now, doubtless, necessary for enjoyment, as well as the development of his faculties, that he be actively engaged. The present world is but a type of that which is to come, in some respects. From what the human spirit is capable of here, clogged, as it is, with its mortal companion, we may have but little conception of its capacity when it shall have an eternal state, in which, forever, to expand its God-given powers.

One great source of enjoyment will be to unravel the dispensations of God's providence, which is now, confessedly, a mysterious subject. "Clouds and darkness are round about Him;" but the shining light of eternity will enable us to see "the end of the Lord" in those things which now seem to be so dark and mysterious. We now walk by faith; but then it will be lost in sight, and hope in glorious fruition, when the glorious realities of the spiritual world burst upon him.

He now, for the first time, sees things in their true light.

The soul is now free from its clay tenement, and enters upon the reward for the deeds done in the body. He will find those around him whose moral nature will correspond with his own. If he has no moral fitness for the pure and the good, he must, of necessity, dwell with the vicious and the vile. We make, in this present state, our place and state of being in the other world, and that, too, by a law which we believe extends throughout the universe of intelligent beings. We make our residence in the other world by the character we form in this. In vain may any one dream of finding a heaven anywhere in the immensity of space, unless they have the kingdom of heaven within them. There is a profound philosophy in this truth, as will be seen and acknowledged by all.

CHAPTER X.

"OUTER DARKNESS"—TRANCE.

THAT there is a place as well as a state of punishment, was taught us in our investigations on this subject. It was not a material fire, but a fire that each had kindled in his own bosom. It is the opposite of the heaven within. The same law establishing the one fixes the other, and one state is created as the other. It is first an organic state of the soul, and then an external place or world, produced in correspondence. All created intelligences make their own place after death, in the heaven or hell which they are fitted for by their choice and their moral condition while they remained in their natural state. Disobedience to the divine will, hideous moral deformity, organized forms of hatred and falsity, produce misery. Love is the life of heaven, hatred the life of hell. This hatred is the legitimate result of love of self. The madness and insanity of self-love can not be seen in this world, while the subject of it is the selfish, avaricious man. The wicked man is surrounded with as many external restraints as the law and his reputation impose upon him. After death, when the spirit acts without such external bonds, it rushes headlong into the wildest excesses, to possess all things, and to rule over all things, and turns with hatred and revenge against every object which seems to stand in the way of its inordinate lusts. "Art thou come hither to torment us?" exclaimed one of these evil ones to Jesus.

This fire of self-love in the heart, engendering pride, hatred, contempt, scorn, revenge, malice, cruelty, and all evil passions, is the hell-fire which torments the wicked. This awful fire is one they have chosen for themselves. They have no moral fitness for heaven, nor could they be happy if they were in the society of the pure and good. There is sound philosophy in a heaven and a hell. An assemblage of such persons as above described would constitute a place of punishment, properly represented by the fearful pictures, drawn by the inspired writers, of "outer darkness," for which alone they are qualified.

We were invited out one evening to Mrs. Winchester's, some two miles from the city. What purported to be the spirit of an old resident of Memphis took possession of her, and gave the most fearful description of his condition I ever heard. He said he was engaged in business there, many years since; that he had cheated and defrauded the widow and the orphan, and that his children were then living off of his ill-gotten gains, while he was suffering indescribable agony for his conduct. He said he had occupied a high position in the community, and been a member of three churches; but in all he was a hypocrite, and was now reaping the reward of his doings. He would rave as a maniac, and threaten death to us, if in his power to inflict it. Several times he called for water. It was the most fearful scene I ever witnessed, and such as I hope never to see again.

I verily believe it to have been a similar case to some of those demons cast out of persons by our Saviour in Judea. The New Testament writers state the fact of possession by demons as one of common occurrence, and not the least marvelous. Many do not believe there are demons or obsessions in this day. Science, some think, has almost driven such things out of the world. They profess to occupy the materialistic heights, far above the weakness of believing in demons. Even some believers in Christianity may sneer at being possessed of evil spirits; but my conviction is that there are now those living who are controlled by wicked, lying spirits, upon the great principle of affinity, the one for the other. I think it is a law of the spiritual world that they can take possession of those whose natures are like their own, upon the same principle, now, as they did in the days of Jesus and the apostles. The spirits whom our Saviour cast out talked with him, some of them desiring to be permitted to go into the swine.

Good people have good spirits to minister to them, while bad people have evil spirits, who seek to control them. This great principle forms the basis of association in this world, and I think it probable that it extends to all created intelligences throughout the universe, as the great law of association, and constitutes the philosophy of our future state of happiness or misery. The pure in heart only shall see or enjoy God. Without this qualification no real happiness can be found in the eternal world. The want of it necessitates the being "driven away in his wickedness," because of utter disqualification for heaven.

This view, I think, is not only scriptural, but fully justifies the ways of God to man, as no other theory can. Our

Heavenly Father is not willing that any should perish; but they cannot be saved while evil and impurity exist within their natures; it is morally impossible.

During the time of our meetings, a gentleman of high standing drowned himself in the Mississippi River. His body was recovered, and brought to Wesley Chapel, where I preached his funeral to a large audience. The first meeting after that, it was announced that he was there, in deep distress. He said that he was present at his funeral, and heard all I said on that occasion; that he tried to control me, and that if he could have done it, that I "would have horrified the congregation by describing the awful sufferings he was enduring" for the crime he had committed, in putting an end to his existence. He begged me to pray for him, asked us to get down upon our knees then, and pray for him. I did not believe in praying for such cases, consequently did not comply with his request. I mention this as one of the incidents of which I know nothing except what transpired at our meeting.

One night after this, at one of the meetings appointed by Mystery at my house, to see what he could do with our servant-girl, before referred to, she seemed to be alarmed, and said she saw a black man. The next morning, when I went into the city, I called on Miss F., when Mystery wrote that "the dark spirit the girl saw last night was the suicide."

From all the investigations I have made of this subject, I have nothing to warrant the belief that the wicked will not be punished in the spirit world, as the Bible says, "according to the deeds done in the body." The nature and extent of that punishment will not be such as I have often heard described from the pulpit.

I find the following in a lecture recently delivered by Mr. Peebles, a celebrated spiritual lecturer, on that subject. "The lessons and principles taught by the invisible intelligences revealed the certainty of just and adequate punishment for sin. No mortal could escape from the consequences of his acts.

"All have their guardian spirits, and no one could hide his secrets from the searching eyes of angels. It was good to confess and forsake sin, to return blessing for cursing, to live kind, forgiving, and loving lives."

We shall find, when the light of the eternal world shines upon us, that a heaven and a hell are the necessary states of being in the other life—that there is an eternal fitness in the one as well as the other. Both are the necessary conditions of the future state of being. All will see and acknowledge that they have had mercy sweetly blended with justice, and all will fully justify the ways of God to them.

TRANCE, OR MAGNETIC STATE.

There is what is called being in trance mentioned in the Old and New Testaments. I think it is a suspension of the "outward man," or senses, and the exercise of the faculties of the "inner man." I have frequently seen persons thus, as science calls it, magnetized. The servant-girl to whom I have referred was sometimes in that condition. Her eyes were closed, her muscles became rigid, and every outward sense seemed to be suspended. While in that state, she would say she saw persons, some of whom she knew, others she did not know. She would describe them minutely, talk to them freely, and tell us what they said, in answer to questions by us. She could never have seen or heard of anything of the kind, and was incapable of deception; nor did she know, when it passed off, what had transpired. I have seen persons, under religious excitement, appear for hours to be in a state of insensibility, who would relate very remarkable things which they saw and heard while in that condition. Thousands of cases are occurring where persons near death see those whom they recognize as their relatives and friends around them, who have passed on before, who are waiting to receive and welcome the loved one to their blissful abode. The angels around the rich man's gate carried Lazarus to the bosom of Abraham. Scenes of this kind have been joyfully witnessed in many families all over the land. They bring consolation to the afflicted that words can not describe. This has occurred in my own family, but it is too sacred for me to mention in this connection. I expect to realize it myself when I come to pass away from the material and enter upon the spiritual state of existence.

How wonderful, how beautiful it is, that both kinds of senses, the spiritual and the natural, can be kept open at the same time!—that one can look from their double eyes into both worlds, hear with their double ears the music of each! While loved ones of earth are singing the songs of Zion around the bedside, the angelic choir, composed of loved ones who have passed over, sings the songs of welcome to the departing one. They can have conversation on earth and "conversation in heaven" at the same time. This may seem, to those who have never investigated this subject, as impossible, and those who believe it deluded; but I have, for many years, had demonstrations clear to my mind that there are thousands of such cases all over the land. Seventeen years since, in Memphis, twelve of its citizens, representing as intellectual and as moral a class as usually meet together, were fully satisfied with the truth of what I have stated. A native-born Memphian, while in a trance, or magnetic state, conversed with our guardian spirits, and told each of us who they were. She gave a minute description of each of them—told what they said to us—while we asked many questions, to which they replied, demonstrating their presence and knowledge of the relations we had sustained to each other, referring to events known only to the parties to whom they were addressed.

Our conviction was that while in that state she saw with her spirit eyes, and heard with her spirit ears, the spirits of those of our relatives who were there. This I think was demonstrated to each of us by personal allusions made known perhaps to none but ourselves. We were profoundly impressed with the truth of the trance, or magnetic state. I have known quite a number of persons in their normal state who possess the same faculty. There are several of them residing in Memphis at this time, who do not belong to that class called spiritualists, but who say they see often, and converse freely with their relatives who have been dead for years. Many, no doubt, will ridicule this, and say they are deranged for saying it, and that I am crazy for writing it. Well, so be it. It is a principle of the intellect that it is not capable of knowing of its derangement, hence such are entitled to sympathy instead of ridicule or sarcasm. They are honest and sincere, and so am I in what I say. What is truth, will ever remain true, notwithstanding the sneers of the unbelieving. If these persons have not the gift of "discerning spirits," mentioned by St. Paul in his Epistle to the Corinthians, I can not tell what that gift to which he refers means. They hear the heavenly music of paradise, and converse with those who have passed over the river of death not in "circles" or "seances," but in their offices, and while engaged in their domestic duties during the day as well as in the quiet of the evening shades.

Thomas Lay, member of Friends Church, was esteemed for his great piety, blameless life, and sincerity of soul. A compilation of his writings and manuscripts were published in Philadelphia in 1796 by Budd and Bertram. I copy two paragraphs of one of his spiritual experiences. Fasting and secret prayer ever proved efficacious in opening his inner sight, enabling him to behold with rapturous joy the marvelous glories of the heavenly world. He says "I thought I had been dead and gone to heaven. After I left my body I heard, as it were, the voices of men, women, and children singing songs of praise unto the Lord God without intermission, which ravished my soul, and threw me into transports of joy. My soul was also delighted with most beautiful glades and gardens, which appeared to me on every side, and such as were never seen in this world. Through these I passed, being clothed in white and in my full shape without the least diminution of parts. As I passed along toward a higher state of bliss, I cast my eyes (being perfectly conscious) upon the earth, which I saw plainly, and beheld three men (whom I knew) die. Two of them were white, one of which entered into immediate rest. There appeared a beautiful transparent gate opened, and as I, with the one that entered into rest, came up to it, he stepped in; but as I was about to enter I stepped into the body. When I recovered from my trance I mentioned the names of these persons, telling where I saw them die, and which of them entered into rest. I said to my mother, Oh, that I had made one step farther, then I should not have come back to earth. After telling them what I had, I desired them to say no more; for I still heard the voices and melodious songs of praise, and longed for my final change.

"After I told them of the death of the three men, they sent to see if it was so. And when the messenger returned, he told them they were all dead, and died in their rooms, as I had told them. Upon hearing it I fell into tears, and said, Oh, Lord, would thou hadst kept me, and sent him back that was in pain (for he seemed to be one of the lost). The third was a colored man, belonging to the Widow Kearney, whom I saw die in the brick kitchen; and while they were laying his corpse on a board; his head fell out of their hands; which I plainly saw, with other circumstances—for I remember the walls were no hinderances to my sight. Though the negro's body was black, his soul was clothed in white; which filled me with joy, as it appeared to me a token of his acceptance with God. Yet I was not permitted to see him fully enter into rest; for, just as I thought myself entering, I came into the body again.

"Some time after my recovery, the Widow Kearney, the mistress of the colored man, sent for me, and inquired whether I thought departed spirits knew one another; I answered in the affirmative, telling her I saw the negro man die while I was lying as a corpse. She then asked 'Where did he die?' I told her in the brick kitchen between the jamb of the chimney and the wall, and that, when they took him from the bed to lay him on the board, his head slipped from their hands. She then said, 'so it did.' She then asked if I could tell where they laid him. I informed her, between the back door and the street door. She said that she remembered that was so, and was satisfied, having reason to believe, what she had often thought, that the departed spirits knew each other in heaven.

"These men, upon inquiry, were found to die at the very time I saw them; and all the circumstances of their death were found to be exactly as I had related them. As some may desire to know how, or in what shape, these that were dead appeared to me, I would say that they appeared each in a complete body, which I take to be the spiritual body, separated from the earthly, sinful body. They were also clothed; the two that entered into rest in white; and the other, who was seemingly cast off, had his garment somewhat white, but spotted. I saw also the bodies in which each of them lived upon earth, and also how they were laid out; but my own body I did not see. The reason why I neither saw my own body, nor entered fully into rest, I take to be this, that my soul was not quite separated from my body as the others were; though it was so far separated as to permit my seeing those things, and hearing their songs of praise and thanksgiving. Some may think the dead know not each other. These I would refer to the Scriptures, asking, Did not Dives know both Abraham and Lazarus, though afar off?"

I have copied this as one of the thousands of cases that occurred long before these modern manifestations, and among the Quakers, a people distinguished for integrity, simplicity, and devotion to religious convictions.

I have conversed with persons who had similar experiences, who were as reliable, every way, as any persons I have ever known. They do not wish their names to be made public, knowing that they would be the subjects of ridicule, in the present state of public opinion upon this subject.

I will, however, give one more case illustrating the same principle.

I knew a man in Christ, about fourteen years ago, whether in the body, I can not tell; or whether out of the body, I can not tell; God kneweth, such a one caught up to the third heaven.

And I knew such a man, whether in the body or out of the body I can not tell; God knoweth. How that he was caught into paradise, and heard unspeakable words which it is not lawful for a man to utter.

The Apostle Paul was elevated to the third heaven, and saw and heard things which were not lawful for him to mention. He was sorely puzzled, and declares that whether in the body or out of it, he could not tell. His sensations told him he was in the body, but his theoretic faculty demanded to know, how he could be in the third heaven, with angels, and still retain all his natural faculties and sensation? He "looked at the things not seen" by mortal eye, as all will, when their natural eye becomes dim in death, and the spiritual eye opens upon the glories of the spiritual world around, into which they have passed.

CHAPTER XI.
SPIRITUAL MANIFESTATIONS.

I THINK the Bible warrants the belief that communications between the natural and the spiritual world have existed from the beginning. There are laws regulating the intercourse between this world and the next that we do not understand; yet the law is as universal as any other law. Under the influence of this law, certain men and women have exercised spiritual powers and gifts. The apostle has, I think, reference to these when he enumerates, among others, " the discerning of spirits." There occurred an extraordinary development of such powers in the first century of the Christian era, the effect of which was to attract attention to the teachings of a system, the innate beauty, and moral grandeur of which far surpassed anything ever known in the world's history. Life and immortality were brought to light by the Gospel of our Lord Jesus Christ, by which "a manifestation of the Spirit was given to every man to profit withal." The existence of such spiritual gifts is traceable throughout the history of the past, and similar gifts and powers show themselves among us at the present time. The phenomena occurring daily under the eye of thousands confirm the truth of this position. They also corroborate the history of these things as recorded in the Old and New Testament Scriptures.

The consciousness of this great truth has impelled me to give utterance to my conviction, through various public channels, for the last seventeen years.

We find neither in the Gospels nor the Epistles a word to indicate the cessation of them in the future of spiritual gifts. So far as there is expression on the subject, they sustain the belief in their indefinite continuance. When our Saviour appeared unto the eleven, he said, "These signs shall follow them that believe. In my name shall they cast out devils; they shall speak with new tongues." These promises are not restricted, but are to all who believe. The Acts of the Apostles are filled with passages in proof of their continuance throughout the apostolic age. Of spiritual powers and gifts, St. Paul declares "there are diversities of gifts, but by the same spirit."

There are many of these manifestations recorded in the Bible. Why is it not as easy to believe that spirits can communicate with men now as anciently? We can not question the one, nor need we doubt the other. Human testimony is used for ancient as well as modern manifestations. If man ever had intercourse with spirits, it was in accordance with a law which has never been abolished. There are, no doubt, certain physiological and psychological conditions necessary for these manifestations, else all men could commune with spirits. The same faculty which aided them to see and commune with spirits anciently, can, if rightly developed, aid them now; and the modern are as real as the ancient ones. These manifestations, when properly understood, come to the aid of the Church, while many of its ministers and members reject them. It supplies to atheists and infidels the lacking evidence of immortality, and they receive it and rejoice in the consolation it brings them. It thus resembles Christianity in its reception, which was rejected by professedly religious men. The doctrine of immortality must ultimately rest upon proof, or be rejected. The tendencies of the present age is to reject everything which can not be demonstrated. Hence, I think, God has given us these things that all may know the truth. If all the phenomena attending the modern movement be accounted for on physiological grounds, without the intervention of spirits, ancient phenomena will have to pass the same ordeal, and receive the same sentence by scientific men. Little as some think of it who ridicule these things, there is more at stake than they have ever imagined. Whatever psychological law will account for involuntary polyglot speaking and writing, modernly, will account for the speaking in unknown tongues, anciently, among those who doubt the direct inspiration given anciently. Whatever psychological law will account for the apparitions, or the seeing of spirit lights, hearing of music, and all those phenomena attested by millions, will account for similar things recorded in the Bible. Whatever psychological law will account for the lifting and moving of tables, pianos, etc., will explain many of the things mentioned in sacred history. Whatever psychological law will account for the numerous cases where spirits have been seen to leave their earthly bodies, wafted upward by a convoy of angels, as Lazarus was, will account for the translation of Enoch and Elijah, and the ascension of our Saviour from Mount Olivet, when "two men" spoke to the multitude who witnessed his departure and his second coming. In rejecting these phenomena, there is more involved than many suppose. God's laws, like himself, are immutable, unchangeable. They are the same now that they were when the "men" talked with Abraham and Lot in regard to God's purposes, developing a principle in his moral government by which the cities of the plain might have been saved. They are the same now that they were when the "man" appeared to Cornelius, and told him to send for Peter, who preached the first Gospel sermon to the Gentiles at his house. And when "the man of Macedonia" appeared unto Paul saying, "Come over into Macedonia and help us," he went over the sea and planted churches there, to whom he addressed epistles received now as part of the canonical books of the New Testament. Let us then, brethren in the ministry, friends of Bible Christianity, meet this question as its importance demands. We can not, we dare not, ignore the facts of these manifestations. The phenomena are too well attested to admit of doubt or cavil. They are, as I verily believe, in perfect accordance with the universal law of God, as it existed from the beginning. I can not believe that law has ever been revoked or changed; neither can I believe that the ancients were more favored in these manifestations than those of the present age. We have nothing leading us to any such conclusion in the Bible, nor is it to be found in any of the laws or principles of nature with which we are acquainted. We know nothing of retrograde movement anywhere, but ONWARD and UPWARD—development everywhere—in the kingdom of grace as well as of nature.

This age is marked more than any other for the development of physical science, and the bringing of the vast resources of nature in subjection to the powers of man.

These laws have been ever since the great Architect of the universe brought it into existence. So in the spiritual world; spiritual laws have ever been established. When in the simplicity and purity of the patriarchal age "angels" or "men" walked and talked with them face to face, without any of that foolish fear which many now have of such intercourse, so in every age, as the conditions were more or less favorable, have been the manifestations to the denizens of earth. There is, I believe, universal agreement among those who have written upon the prophicies of the Scriptures, that the present age is to be characterized by the most remarkable events which have ever occurred in the world's history. Some believe it to be one thing, some another, but all agree that we are upon the eve of important events in the moral world. What these are, we can not tell. All, from their standpoint, may have their opinion of the shadows which coming events are casting before them.

I can not but look upon these remarkable spiritual manifestations, occurring all over the civilized world, without believing that they are the harbinger of a brighter day that is to dawn upon the world, when immortality shall indeed be brought to light by the Gospel

Having given my opinion so fully and freely, all through what I have written upon this subject, as to the fallibility of what is received by these communications, I need not repeat, that I try what comes through that channel just in the same way I would that which comes from those in the present world. There, as well as here, there is great diversity of opinion upon the various doctrines, principles, and experiences of those in the spiritual world. Hence, I have ever followed the advice given at our circle, to reject everything that was not in accordance with the doctrines and principles taught in the Bible. This I regard as the only safe ground to occupy on this question. With this blessed book, as our chart, and the Lord Jesus Christ as our "chief corner-stone," forming the basis upon which we rear our glorious superstructure, with the love of God in the heart, and a universal love to our fellow-men, we can not materially err. Purity of heart, and holiness of life, are the essential requisites for admittance into the paradise of God, as taught by good spirits as well as the revelation of his written word in the Old and New Testament Scriptures. There is harmony between them; and a profound philosophy in their teachings which force conviction upon every candid, reflecting mind.

There were those in the apostolic day (Acts xxiii. 9), who said, "We find no fault in this man, but if a spirit or an angel had spoken unto him, let us not fight against God."

I would respectfully suggest to those who think it their duty to *oppose, deny, and ridicule* these things, to examine the Scriptures, as the noble Bereans did, "to see if these things are not so." If ever they have occurred, why may they not occur again; and on ever the same? May they not be found fighting against what God designs to be a most glorious privilege conferred upon man?

Gamaliel's advice to those who were clamoring for the destruction of the apostles, might be taken by some to advantage. "If it be of man it will come to naught, but if it be of God, you can not destroy it."

CLOSING MEETING OF THE CIRCLE.

I could fill many pages respecting the physical manifestations at our meetings, for the gratification of visitors; but these amount to but little after they are once witnessed. The performance on the guitar, with no visible hand touching it, and the piano keeping time by rising up, no one being near it, only as the medium, who knew nothing of music, touched the keys, were of some interest to us. Our time was not spent with such things except for the gratification of others.

A child of Mr. King's, at whose house we met, died during the time, and I preached its funeral. In the morning the door bell commenced ringing, and continued to ring until we left with the child for the cemetery. It is unnecessary to mention anything further of physical manifestations. Those who never have seen such things, will not, perhaps can not, believe them. Such is the constitution of most minds, that they require occular demonstration before they can believe that such things do occur.

Having some of the last writings of Mystery, I insert them to show the character of what he taught us. If they are not in accordance with the Bible, then I am not capable of forming a correct opinion of them.

Every Man has a Talent.

FROM MYSTERY TO HENRY KING.

"*Question.* Has not every one a talent?

"*Ans.* Did not the great Teacher say, 'Every man hath a talent for which he must account in the next world. Like the slothful servant, should he bury it in the deep darkness of the second sphere, must he grope for it; and, in his agony, return to earth, until, amid the ruins of a misused life, he finds it hidden with rust, caused by wicked deeds and horrid acts. And even then he has it to purify and use until it becomes clean, beautiful, and bright as when, a jewel from the hand of the great Master Workman, it was placed in this clay casket. Yes, live not for this world, but for the better land. Lay not up for yourselves treasures on earth, but above, where you shall find them when you go hence.

"You now have two bright gems there which will shine as the stars forever and forever. They were but little ones here, only missed in your home, around your board; but in heaven, or rather in the spirit land, they hold high places. Little lambs, gathered early to the shepherd's fold; no earth stains rest on them; and with shouts of joy would they welcome you up on high. Come one, come all. Jesus died not for one man nor for one nation, but for all nations, for all men; and he who dies early knows the love of Jesus in another world if he can not understand it here. These communications are for you; for should we never meet on earth, that is, should you never see me write again, remember, though all your earth friends should desert you, there is one on high who will never forsake his children; and through the world wherever you may roam, I will be with you each day, and if in trouble will try to pour the balm of consolation in your soul. Yea, I will, if God wills it, be with you in the hour of death. When earth fades in the distance and doubts arise as to your future state, Christ shall take your hand and say, 'Fear not, for I am with you.' Then the bright light of love shall fall upon your soul, and you shall rejoice and know for a certainty that you have a home in a better land. The Bible must be your study; its pages will become more beautiful to you, and you shall there find the knowledge you wish, if you will but read—not one chapter or one page, but page after page, chapter after chapter, until it will be the Book of all books to you, and Christ the man of your counsel. Yea, you shall be a Christian— a living example of what man can be. Then will an aged mother feel her prayers are at last answered—her long lost son is found indeed; and when, at last, you sit down with Abraham, Isaac, and Jacob, in your Father's home, that mother will be there, and with tears of joy will she tell unto you her deep, heart-felt anxiety on earth for you. Then shall your children look back and say, 'Yea, our father was in very truth a Christian.' Oh, man, what an inheritance to leave your little ones when you are gathered home!—a life that in serving God, a chart for them to steer by—a claim to the heavenly Jerusalem. They are young: even now speak to them of things heavenly, their little eyes sparkle, and they ask, 'Papa, can I go there?' Then you may be able to say, 'Yes, my child, for Christ has said, 'I am the way, the truth, and the light, whosoever cometh unto me I will in nowise cast out.' Yes, read your Bible; there you will find God's will concerning man. You will, I know, take but little interest at first, but it will increase with each day's perusal, until it will be a part of your daily food. Now, read what I have here written, treat it not lightly, for 'tis of eternal interest to your eternal, never-dying soul."

FROM FANNY KING TO HER BROTHER.

"I do not wish you to understand that all can reign in

glory. Ah, no! Christ died, that all who loved him should inhabit that glorious abode which he has gone to prepare; but those who are willing in this life to serve God, they shall inherit a most glorious home on high; they shall sit down with Abraham in their Father's kingdom, and with hundreds of redeemed souls, shall make the vaults of heaven resound with their song of praise to the most high God. After leaving our earthly abode, we can see the mourners who gather around our old form—we wonder that you should love it so well. How different with us. We feel as a captive bird let loose from its prison cage; and you should rejoice with us, to think when a soul leaves this earth—remember there is then another throne filled on high, another harp resounds to the praises of God. For here we are still progressing in our studies and praising God, till we are made perfect by our own exertions and the divine grace of Jesus Christ; then we may enter that glorious abode of God, of which you can never know till you receive your new harp and your heavenly robes from the hands of Him who died, that you might be an heir of God, and a joint heir with him to that glorious kingdom which my frail words can not describe. This generation has not advanced far enough to speak to us, but in years to come, the mist which now shrouds this great phenomena, will have passed away, and all will be able to communicate with their departed friends. But you who now possess the privilege of even this slow way of communication, should improve it, for millions of dollars are composed of cents, and if you do not appreciate this small privilege, would you be any more grateful if your powers were increased? But you can only progress little by little. If you cultivate and strive to make good use of the powers which some few now possess, the powers will be increased, and with them the day of wonders shall never cease, till they are called to give an account of the deeds done in the body. Then, and not till then, will they find how great has been the powers bestowed upon them, and then will they reflect how great has been the abuse of that power; for, like the slothful servant, they will have hidden their talent in the earth, when, if they had used it for a good purpose, great would have been their reward. In the beginning God intended that after a few years of earthly pleasure, man should enjoy an eternity with him in heaven, a place far surpassing this world, in grandeur and scenes pleasing for the eye to rest upon; but Adam fell, and man continued to sink lower and lower, till one of the attributes of God descended from his throne on high and became man, and dwelt among them. And because he came not as an earthly monarch, with all the wealth of an Eastern prince, he was mocked and spit upon, and died the ignominious death of the cross; but by his death all men have now a free access to a heavenly home. He came to again make clear the path which had so long remained closed, the road which leads to the very King eternal. His name is the pass-word which will lead us to glory. Each prayer which ascends to heaven must be indorsed, as it were, with the name of Jesus Christ; for unless we plead in his name our prayers will remain unanswered. In the beginning there was no spiritual world, for man was made perfect on earth; but after Adam's fall man became so low that he forgot the very existence of a God; and after Christ's coming souls were fitted for heaven in the spirit world by angels sent by our heavenly Father to prepare us for the enjoyments of heaven. And after leaving the seventh sphere we can not commune with man—we forget then all earthly things, our thoughts are of God and heavenly pleasures, which differ widely from earthly enjoyments. And now I would ask, Why does man love this body so well? for, like the egg-shell, it is only intended to protect the more delicate interior; and after death, like the new-born bird, we lay down this earthly covering, and in a more heavenly form we ascend to the place which is intended for the redeemed. But now let me say to you here, there is an abode prepared for the wicked, those who have lived in open rebellion before God; a place where the smile of God is forever shut out. But not till they have had many opportunities to turn to Christ are they thus punished. Speak, speak to those around you who are fast approaching this dreary abode, and remember, he who turns a sinner from the error of his way shall save a soul from death and hide a multitude of sins. And to you, my dear brethren, I would say, You have just begun a good work, but faint not till you have gained that land where the sun never rises nor sets, but where the countenance of God illumines all around; for it is brighter than the sun and more mild than the rays of a summer's moon."

Having given the foregoing communications, which, though personal, have some principles of general application, I now give the reader the last which we had from Mystery, addressed to us as a circle. He said:

"Not that I wish to leave you, oh, no. There is not one of the circle whom I do not love; and though thousands of miles may separate you, once a day will Mystery be with you. Though years may pass before you are called home, I shall meet you at the river, and you shall pass its waves without a struggle, for I shall hold your hand, and the River of Death will have no terror to you; for in the distance you shall see your new home, and the light of the heavenly spheres shall break upon you.

"To you, my little band, my chosen few, who amid rain and heat came to me for instructions, I would say, God-speed you who have been faithful, and forget not to assemble yourselves together, and I will try and develop some of you as mediums. You shall have glorious manifestations, and many shall wonder at your instructions.

"To Mr. Watson I would say, Don't give your girl up. She will be a good medium, and so will another servant-girl of yours, a female much older than the one not practiced with. But, oh, give it not up now. Spiritualism is only in its infancy, let it not go until it is able to stand of itself. Do not put your hands to the plow and then look back, but move on, and a glorious harvest shall be yours, and a crown at the right hand of His Majesty on high shall be yours. To Drs. Pittman and Taylor I would say, Faint not by the wayside. You must not give up now, for you will hereafter rejoice over these times of doubts, and be glad that you struggled through this cloud of doubt; for bright and glorious will be the day which shall follow its departure. Go on! And to Carr and King I would say, You both do well, and even now feel the influence for good which surrounds you. To King I would say, Do not build your hopes too high on becoming a medium, for you may be disappointed, but you will never regret the day you became a CHRISTIAN SPIRITUALIST; for you will, in years to come, be glad, and in eternity you shall often look back with pleasant thoughts to the hours that you have spent around the board with Mystery as a teacher. To Dr. Howcott I would say, Do not give up, but go on. And to Dr. Gilbert I will say, You carry in your daily life the proofs that this doctrine has done you good. And now farewell. And when you and I stand face to face in heaven, you shall know for truth who Mystery is, and who he was, and why it was that he was sent to you as a teacher.

"I will write for you some other time. So now, farewell. Go on in this great and glorious work."

MYSTERY'S PARTING COUNSEL.

"Hold that which is good, that which will stand in the light of the Gospel. If once you receive a communication which will not accept Jesus as the Son of God, have done with that spirit, for he is not one of us. He is bringing you no good; but all who own Christ as the Son of God receive them, and their teachings will do you good.

"It is to be my last night with you, it may be for months, it may be forever—for who but God can tell where you shall be before to-morrow's sun shall set; but an all-wise Father rules on high, he will direct you if you will but ask his aid. 'Fear not, little flock, for 'tis your father's good pleasure to give you the kingdom.' Yea, fear not, with Jesus for your guide, and myriads of spirits to assist you, you can not fail to reach the upper spheres. My interest for you is very great, and 'tis with sorrow that I see my little circle break up; but as I have fixed an hour in each day I will be with you; and were it in a congregation of a thousand, I shall know if any are there who are of this little band, who, though others have laughed, have feared not the scorn of men. In years to come you will, or, if God wills it otherwise, your children shall read of your labors here, and many shall rise up and call you blessed. I did hope all would be present to-night, but I suppose it could not be. Meet as you promised as often as you can, for Christ hath said, 'Where two or three are met together in my name, there shall I be in the midst of them.'

"Fear not, for I too will meet with you when I can. But remember, oh, man, we are but disembodied spirits; at times we give only our opinions; we, like you, may be wrong. We look not into the future only by the signs of the times. Do not expect too much from us; we will try to do our part. When dangers surround you I will be with you, and if I can not do away with it, will try to alleviate your pain. Yea, thousands upon thousands look down and smile on this circle; fathers and mothers, brothers and sisters, parents and children watch around with anxious eye, fearing you will not receive this great truth.

7

Look at it in the proper light. Spirits, yea, the very spirits that once inhabited the clay form, and walked over this green earth, when once in the spirit world, return, that you, knowing the way, may walk therein. We, who have passed through the torment and agony of the second sphere, return to you that you may shun it. Ah, man! the deepest midnight darkness of earth is broad, beautiful sunlight in comparison to that. Then not only the darkness without, but the deep darkness within the soul—not one ray of light, hope gone, what is the poor, lost spirit to do? He sees a light, he hears earth voices. Swift, as on the lightning's flash, does he speed to that little ray. 'Tis around a circle of the children of earth. Why do they gather around that table? why do they listen with such deep anxiety to each little rap? Joy, joy, 'tis a spirit that speaks to them! Ah, yes, they see this. Then, thinks this dark spirit, lo, there is a world of spirits above me. How can I gain that upper land? Is it dark there too? Hark, that bright spirit says there is no night there, all is joy and peace. Yes, I will listen, I will learn; and so they do. So they progress until they reach the fourth sphere; there they have spirit teachers, face to face.

"So you see, oh, man! 'tis not only you, the twelve that sit around this table who are instructed, but hundreds who have gone before, and who with joy watch each word as it falls from my pencil. But remember, 'tis not only to hear, but by your living example let the world know you are none of these. If there is truth in this thing it will stand through all ages. Was not Christianity nursed in a cloud and cradled in a storm? so it will be with Spiritualism; but it shall come forth doubly purified by the fire, and all men shall believe and rejoice in it. For then will Jesus, the much-despised Nazarine, reign over the whole earth; and oh! 'tis Mystery's prayer that some at this table may live to see it; for earth will be a heaven.

"The ball is in motion, it will roll the spacious earth around, and with one great shout, resounding through heathen as well as Christian lands,—that spirits of the blessed do return to teach poor man. Yes, there are hundreds who will not receive the Gospel, who reject the Son of God, who say death is a long, dark, everlasting sleep; but the spirits will remove all this, we will give them such proof as will remove every doubt, and they will then begin to think of a preparation for hereafter. But delay not, now is the accepted time, now is the day of salvation. 'Work while the day lasts, for the night cometh when no man can work.' Yea, work and you shall receive a rich reward in that upper and better world. In the hour of trial I will be with you. Fear not, little flock, for 'tis my mission to you that you shun the second sphere. I would have you shine as bright stars in the seventh sphere. Ah! remember there is a world beyond the spheres, where you shall see God, for you shall be like him. Ah! the Jordon is to be crossed by you, spirits bright and beautiful will guide you to the banks, and angels of God will receive you on the other side, there to dwell with God forever. Ah! yes, with angels as your companions, God as a father, how will the ages of eternity pass! Yes, you must, you can shun the dark world, where one day appears as a thousand years. Yes, you can reign with God forever if you will but take the Bible as your guide and Christ for your example. He came down to earth for man's good; he left the realms of glory that man, knowing the road, might walk therein. The path, though narrow, is illuminated by his love; the road, though it appeareth long to the children of man, is but a narrow span, which clouds the shores of time with eternity. Dwell in readiness, for in such an hour as ye know not the son of man cometh. Live not for time, but for eternity, so, should you be called at this hour, you would enter the sixth sphere; then I, who have been your teacher on earth, will be your teacher there; then we shall look upon one another, and oh! with what eagerness will you devour my teachings; for when you leave the seventh sphere there is but one more step to the home of God the Father—you may gain that too. Now, may the most choice of God's blessings rest upon you, and may we meet around his throne on high."

Thus terminated the most deeply interesting meetings I ever attended. We most sincerely believed that for several months we had been in communication with a spirit of high order from the better land. His teachings had a most hallowed influence on us, and we closed with great reluctance. I have never been so much benefitted spiritually by any associations I have ever enjoyed. I look back through the lapse of seventeen years with unspeakable joy at what we received during our meetings, and enjoyment while attending them.

I have now given some of the main features of our investigations of this subject, with the doctrines taught and the principles inculcated. I leave the reader to come to whatever conclusion he may see proper from the standpoint he may occupy as an honest inquirer after truth. I know that I have earnestly desired and most fervently prayed that I might know the truth. I can have no motive to deceive others, or desire to be deceived myself. I do not wish to influence others only as the statement of the facts as they occurred with us may lead them to think on these things. Several of the parties who composed our company are still living in Memphis who will attest the truth of what I have written.

CHAPTER XII.

FURTHER INVESTIGATIONS.

Having business that required my attention at the North, before leaving I called on Miss Fisher, to see what might be said to me personally. The following communication was written in what seemed to be a lady's handwriting; after which, on the opposite page, in Mystery's peculiar chirography, was another communication, which I think was the last one I ever received from him.

"I am with you, my son. Although taken while you were but a little child, I have always thrown my influence around you, and I can with joy say it has not returned to me void. Yes, though you had no earth-mother, a spirit-mother guarded your path. Her white wings of purity (purified in the blood of the Lamb) protected you from many dangers, and kept you from many temptations, and delivered you from evils unknown at the time. Your interest in this matter has been great, but your labor has been smiled upon, and we hail your arrival in the field with joy.

"You will soon leave Memphis. Investigate this subject at the North. There it is more generally known and understood. You will look back upon this summer with pleasure, for you shall open the eyes of men; for their eyes are closed, or they see through a glass but dimly. I, too, have been at your circle—have heard the teachings of Mystery, sometimes received by strangers as pearls cast before swine, but to your circle as gems from another and a better land.

"You have a good medium in your own family. You should make her practice. She will become a good and quite an interesting medium.

"Now, my son, I shall be with you in all your journeyings, and in time of danger will protect you; but trust to One greater than I, for he is the only one on whom you should rely. Well, now farewell.

"SUSANNAH WATSON."

After this the following was written by Mystery:

"Your mother has said 'Farewell,' but you must be prepared to have people contradict your word—tell you that you are crazy, or something else; but the time is coming when all men shall believe. Do not give yourself one uneasy thought; it will all come out right in the end. Christ guards the old ship of Zion, and she shall—yes, she shall—find a safe landing. Many souls shall be on board. Fear not, but trust in Providence, wherever you may be."

I paid little or no attention to the subject after this, only in 1860 Dr. Mansfield was at Memphis, and several prominent members of the church, with myself, were invited to see him, one afternoon. I had never been in any circle only as I have mentioned. I was the first one that arrived at Dr. Gilbert's, where he was stopping. I was shown the way up-stairs to his room. I had never seen him, nor he me, that I know of. He was alone, and I gave no name, but wrote the names of the persons I wished to communicate with privately, and folded the paper over several times. He laid them on a table, and wrote as follows:

"DEAR BRO. WATSON—Think it not strange that I come instead of your darling mother, who is at this moment away on duty. She will be with you soon—have patience, and let us come to you in our own way, and all our power to convince, as to our spirit power to come to you through the source of mortal organization, will be done.

"Your friend and brother, J. D. ANDREWS."

I then wrote, "If it be my friend Andrews, will he give something that will satisfy me of his identity?"—folding and wrapping up the paper as before—when it was written:

"Well, Bro. Samuel, I am not able to say what I could as to those pleasant meetings in 1859; but I well recollect my labors in Dardanelle, Dover, Augusta, and other places in which I labored during my sojourn below. My home is now in the New Jerusalem, though I find it not as I anticipated, yet my anticipations were more than realized. Yes, Bro. Watson, now sent, we communicate with mortals. Be firm, and you shall live to put all opposition under your feet. I say, Stand up to what you feel to be your duty, and you shall be guarded by that host, numbering thousands, to one who shall dare oppose you. My dear wife and children! Speak a word consoling for me. It will do better for you to tell it to them than me. I have more to say to them after awhile.

"Your friend and brother, J. D. ANDREWS."

"MY DEAR SON SAMUEL—Your friend and brother, Andrews, comes for me, saying you would speak with me. Oh, I thank you, my son! How my soul throbs with joy at having this opportunity of speaking with you. Your dear father is present, yet not able to speak to you. He is frantic with joy at knowing you have called for him. Separated from you by what you call death, he will come and say a word by and by.

Samuel, you have a mission to perform, and if you heed its impression, well will it be with you. You was raised up for that which now awaits you. All your success, pecuniarily and otherwise, has been given you or attributed to spirit agency, or with reference to that which yet awaits you; then, as your friend Andrews has said, Be firm, and know we are with you and will sustain you.

"Your spirit mother, SUSANNAH WATSON."

After the above, the following:

"MY DEAR SON—Your mother has kindly given way and not only so, but proffered me the aid of her control to respond to your interrogatory. Now, my son, your mission is to proclaim this great and mighty truth to millions yet in darkness as to the truth of spirit communication. After awhile you will see your way clear. After awhile you will have strength to proclaim what you will feel your duty. Yes, like John the Baptist, will you be called to lead the way.

"I say, my son, watch! for the day is near.

"Your father,   LEVIN WATSON." *

One of my friends who visited Dr. M. desired to have a communication from his "Uncle Allen" (long a prominent member of the Methodist Church in Nashville, at an early day), and received the following:

"MY DEAR BRO. S———: Think it not singular, or consider it not unconscious, of my coming to you unsolicited. I have stood by and witnessed your Uncle Allen's attempts to come to you, even to the crowding away of those you have called for, yet he has failed in his attempt often.

"Now, thank God, you have lived to see this day, to witness what I had so long looked for, but died without seeing it. Well, Bro., try and profit by its warning influence. You will be beset on all sides, and much will be said to dissuade you from this truth or light just dawning on your age; but stand firm. Would that I could come to earth again! I would do differently from what I did while there; but, Bro., I could not, and did not, fully believe in a hereafter. My conduct showed it. You well know this, but I will tell you much after awhile. Your spirit friend and brother,   JOHN NEWLAND MAFFIT."

These things were absorbed by others of a material nature during the war. I paid no further attention to the subject until last year. The old clock in Arkansas, insignificant as it was, arrested my attention as to its striking—being just before four members of my family died. My

---

* My father died in 1857, in his 72d year.

giving an account of this, and Dr. Bond's course in regard to it, has been the occasion of all this being presented to the public. I was not willing to be censured, as I have been for what I wrote, and bear it without reply; and, when denied his columns, this seemed to me to be the only recourse to vindicate myself, and proclaim what I believe to be the truth.

CAN SPIRITS BE SEEN WITH MATERIAL EYES?

I know science (so-called) says they can not. Nothing can be seen that will not cast a shadow. Spirits can not cast a shadow, therefore no mortal eye can see them. Such is the manner of reasoning by some of the would-be wise. I have no time to argue against such sophistry. Many who believe in the Bible doctrine of ministering spirits, do not believe they can be seen.

Those whose mind and time are absorbed by temporal things are not prepared to appreciate and enjoy such things. Their spiritual faculties are closed; they do not see through a glass even darkly, because of the moral film over their eyes. Such, perhaps, never will be able to see until the natural organs of sight cease to perform their office; but there are those whose spiritual vision is at times opened, so that they have at least some glimpses of spirits. I believe it, because the Bible teaches from the beginning to its close that persons did see them under every dispensation. Do they see them now? Thousands of persons affirm that they do. Are they not as reliable as those who lived thousands of years since? We believe them in regard to everything else, why not in regard to this, especially when it is corroborated by the Bible?

I will mention a few cases which have occurred in this vicinity illustrative of this truth. The first Methodist preacher who was ever stationed in this city was subsequently in the city of New Orleans, La. One night he was aroused from his slumbers by what he was satisfied was his mother. He told me a few days since that he heard his mother's voice as clearly and as distinctly as he ever did, saying, "FRANK, MY SON, BE FAITHFUL. I AM AT REST." His mother was living in Middle Tennessee. When he heard from his father, he found his mother had died at that time.

One of our best official members at the First Methodist Church, in this city, related a similar experience to several of us, recently. In six weeks he received a letter from Germany, stating that his mother died the night that she appeared to him in Arkansas.

Those who have read Mr. Wesley's journal, will remember similar cases. One was away out on the ocean, where he died (or was drowned). He appeared at home, told them he had died that night on a certain ship, in such a latitude and longitude. A record was kept of the facts, which were afterward ascertained to be true in every particular.

A judge of this city informed me, a few days since, that in his wife's father's family, a case occured in the daytime. A gentleman whom they knew intimately, came in the room, when he was addressed by his friend, and his wife was told to hand him a chair, but he had vanished out of sight. It was afterward ascertained that he had died just before that time.

A prominent physician, of this city, told me yesterday, that during the war a member of his family appeared, who was in the army, and it was afterward ascertained that he died about that time. He said he had never mentioned it to any one before.

An officer of the Confederate army, who resides in this city, having lost a lovely little daughter at home, found her with him during the war. She continues with him, often visible, affording him much comfort, and an assurance that she lives in the spirit world.

Another friend, whom I have known in this city for over thirty years, has lost several children; he has seen them all, with the colored woman that nursed them, in his room.

A Methodist preacher, who resided at Memphis, who had long been an itinerant, told me he often saw and conversed freely with those who had passed from earth.

One of the most deeply pious and intelligent ladies, that I knew for more than a quarter of a century, told me, a few days since, that her father, mother, and son, who was an officer in the Confederate army, visited her in her room.

I heard one of our oldest and most influential citizens, recently tell one of our editors that he saw and conversed with a brother frequently, and that he was more company for him now than before he died.

A young lady, near me, says the same of her brother, who controls her.

I met two of our most prominent lawyers on the street. One of them said he had lost several children, but they were with him at home—he saw and talked with them often.

Many years ago, there was a young man, by the name of Charlie Dennie, who professed religion and joined the Church, when I was stationed at Asbury Chapel, in this city. He wrote some very fine poetry, which was published in the Memphis *Christian Advocate*, while I edited it, and he was preparing for the ministry. He went to New Orleans on business, and died suddenly. His remains were brought to Memphis, and I preached his funeral at his brother's house. Just before the service commenced, his brother told me that the night Charlie died, he came into his room, and he asked him why he had come back so soon. The next morning a dispatch told of his death.

I know that the relation of these things will subject me to ridicule, but what of that? I have passed beyond that long since. I could relate some things, in my own experience, but they are too sacred to be soiled by the slang of the unthinking portion of the community. They have never realized anything of the kind, and think, as Dr. Bond says, there is a "morbid state of brain" with those who have. They have not examined the subject from a Biblical stand-point, nor perhaps from any other than a sarcastic one, yet they have the unblushing effrontery to condemn those who have. Had they lived in the days of Jesus, they would have said, "Oh, that Transfiguration was only a ghost story for silly people." This may have been the reason why Jesus "charged them that they should tell no man what things they had seen till the Son of Man were risen from the dead." And they kept that saying with themselves. Thus it is with thousands who have realized sensibly the presence of loved ones, but are afraid of the ridicule of those who have no other mode of meeting this question than to apply epithets to those who, perhaps, are as capable of judging of the facts as themselves. I as much believe that people see those who have once lived here, as that Cornelius saw the "man" that appeared to him. I believe as sincerely that spirit hands are now seen, and write, as I believe that a hand wrote Belshazzar's doom upon the wall of his palace. These things are being repeated in the present age, not by anything miraculous, but in accordance with the laws of the spiritual world.

How true are the Preacher's words (Eccl. iii. 15) : "That which has been, is now . . . . and God requireth that which is past." Many are like Job, who says: "Fear came upon me, and trembling, which made my bones shake. Then a spirit passed before my face; it stood still, but I could not discern the form thereof."

We believe Job saw the spirit, yet many who believe Job's testimony profess to doubt any man's veracity who affirms he sees just what Job and many others say they saw thousands of years ago. Ah, consistency, thou art a jewel! Memory, sympathy and love caused their return there; and millions, influenced by the same feelings, cause them to return now. We cannot believe, or disbelieve, as we please. Sufficient evidence compels belief. It is not a mere act of volition. You cannot believe in this spiritual phenomenon without the most positive evidence. Few, comparatively, have had that evidence; hence the reason of doubt among those who have no experience in these things. This is as might be expected. Persons should not be blamed for not believing. It is often said the days of miracles are past. That may be so; but there is nothing miraculous in all these things, as I have often said. It is in accordance with law that has been in existence from the beginning. As in ancient times these manifestations were usually made when the persons to whom they appeared were alone, so it usually is now—in the home circle of private families they make their appearance.

The man who appeared to Manoah's wife met with her several times privately before her husband saw him, when he asked him if he was the man who appeared to his wife, and he said he was. So with many others all through the sacred record.

It is a momentous question. Can, and do our loved ones return, and can we see and converse with them? I assert that they can. 1st, from the authority of the Bible, and the opinion of the most learned and pious commentators; and, 2d, from the testimony of tens of thousands now living.

Multitudes are to be pitied for having neither the inclination nor the manly courage to investigate that which, demonstrating a future conscious existence, takes hold of the vital principles underlying immortality. A degenerate public opinion is the most contemptible tyrant. I thank God I have passed the point to care much about it.

Through all the preaching of the Gospel we find this

light kept alive, enkindling zeal, and making converts to the Christian faith. It seems strange to me that any Christian can ignore these things. The Apostle besought all to covet earnestly spiritual gifts, among which he specially enumerated sight, for it was considered one of the most natural of all gifts. What nonsense would this command be to those who had within them no organs of spiritual sight, and if there were no spiritual objects of vision? The seeing of spirits was considered a help to Christian attainment, and inspired the faith of the individual to meet the opposition of that age.

Being fully persuaded in my own mind that all will know in the other life, if not in this, the truth of these things, I can cheerfully bide my time. Though what I have written may cause many to sympathize with me for my delusion, yet I think I have the truth on my side. Though they may seem incredible to those who have never experienced them, yet they are very precious truths to those who have realized them, and they can and will stand the test of the most rigid investigation, upon the testimony of witnesses of the most unimpeachable veracity and sincerity.

As a further contribution, I extract a very remarkable experience from a pamphlet by the Rev. A. K. MacSorley, a clergyman of the Church of England, and published in 1865. It is entitled, "An Appeal to the Clergy for the Investigation of Spiritualism, with the Personal Experience of the Writer, by one of themselves." Among other interesting experiences narrated is the following, which we have slightly abridged:

"One evening my wife and I were invited to spend the evening with a friend, whose son was one of our mediums. There were eight of us altogether. A seance was held. A paraffin lamp was burning, and we were told by the spirit to lower the light and screen the fire. Then we were bid to mark well the medium's forehead. After a short time all except one of the company saw a light in the medium's forehead.

"The light was about the size of a goose's egg, across his forehead, of a dim nature, not at all bright, but there it was. Shortly afterward the medium was again made to write 'Pray.' We all knelt down, and I prayed aloud, 'Oh Father, grant that we all may be under a good and gracious influence, so that we may receive light and truth, that we may do nothing contrary to thy holy will. Open our brother's eyes that he may also receive light as well as us, to thy honor and glory, for thy name's sake. Amen.' We had no sooner risen from our knees and taken our seats than he said, 'I also see the light.' The medium then wrote on the paper, 'Thank God! you have seen the spirit-light; now we shall be able to show ourselves to you.' I turned up the light, and read out the paper, and then put it down again. After remaining a little longer quiet, the medium again wrote, 'Mr. K., mark well the medium's action from his head to his waist, and keep quiet.' We all sat very quiet, in great expectation, waiting for what was to come. We heard a great rattle like some electrical-machine, and the room began to tremble. The medium stood up, we could see him distinctly, he stood erect, his arms stretched out in the form of a cross; then he lifted his hand to his head, slipping his fingers through his hair some half-dozen times. Presently he turned to the wall and shook hands, apparently, with some one, then he turned right round, and appeared to do the same with some one else, then with another also, then he appeared to embrace a fourth, then shook hands with some one else, and so on for a considerable time, as if he had been meeting with a considerable number of friends, who had all met together for some gladsome occasion. Then, after having saluted them all, he again stood quiet. We could now see from his head to his waist quite clearly—the light was clearer.

Presently his appearance was changed, and there stood before us a man of about middle age, with a bushy beard of sandy color, broad face, high cheek-bones, broad, full forehead, and benevolent countenance.

"He looked round with a pleased air at each of us, and then disappeared. Next came a young, pale, thin-faced man, with no beard and but very little whisker, black hair, and mild, pleasant-looking countenance. He had a pair of bands round his neck, as a clergyman would have at times. I thought I knew him, but to this day I cannot recall him to my recollection. After staying about the same time before us he disappeared, and then a female of a most beautiful appearance took his place. She was standing as if in the attitude of prayer, with a heavenly countenance brightly beaming forth, her eyes looking upward, and her hair nicely done up, as with a coronet, but it was all hair; and she had a sweet flower at one side of her head. My wife cried out, 'Surely I have seen her before. Is she not an actress?' She disappeared, and the medium wrote on a bit of paper, 'No; she was no actress, but a pure and simple-minded girl, who loved her God and her fellow-creatures. Go you and do likewise.' I then turned up the light, read the writing, and again lowered it. The next that came was a female—one that I had good reason to know while she was in the form. As soon as she appeared, the master of the house exclaimed, 'Oh, Mr. K., is that not your daughter?' I replied, 'You forget that my daughter is in the flesh. She is very like her—I know her well.' She came near me and smiled sweetly. My wife knew her at once, having been intimate with her while in the body, and she said to her, 'If you are she whom I think you are, let me know.' She drew near to her, and stooped down quite close to her, bowing her head and smiling. She stopped with us longer than any of the others, and after again bowing, disappeared. She was my first wife, and the mother of her, Mr. S. thought, she was so like. After she went, we saw one after another, male and female, as many as three dozen. All seemed heavenly and happy, apparently delighted that they could thus manifest themselves to us. When all had gone, the medium wrote again, 'Now, Mr. K., we have fulfilled our promise to you. We have shown you one third of our circle. The arrangements were not prepared for the others to show themselves. Go on and let the truth be known, and we shall be with you. Good night.'"

I copy from a letter written by Judge Edmunds to the New York *Tribune:* "My next step was to see an individual spirit, that of an old friend who had been dead six or eight years. I was in my room at work, not thinking of him, and suddenly I saw him sitting by my side, near enough for me to touch him. I perceived I could exchange thoughts with him, for, in answer to my questions, he told me why he had come. During all these steps of progress I could converse with spirits whom I saw, as easily as I could with any living mortal, and I held discussions with them as I have with mortals."

The time is coming, and I think not far distant, when these things will not be so rare as they are now. There are many now who enjoy them, which gives them the best assurance of immortality. Faith to them has performed its office—" the invisible appears in sight," and the loved and the lost are seen and recognized by mortal eyes. It brings to my mind and heart that which is unspeakably joyful to know, that they watch over us, and "can become visible to mortals" now, as they did in olden time. I have no argument with those who ridicule these things, but simply say, that to my mind it has been demonstrated, beyond the possibility of doubt, that they can and do manifest themselves.

CHAPTER XIII.

THE PHILOSOPHY AND RELIABILITY OF THESE MANIFESTATIONS.

There is an influence which one person can exercise over another by what is called Mesmerism. In this state the external senses seem to be partially asleep, or paralyzed, while the spiritual senses are partially opened. The operator having got his subject completely under his control, can then make him see whatever he chooses. He can project usual images in his own mind by his own will, so that the subject sees objects as external things. Their intense excitement and involuntary gesticulations show unmistakably that they conceive them to be as real, as the outer world is, to the waking perceptions. We were told, in our investigations, that it was upon this principle that spirits operated upon those whose physical organism they could control. They take possession of the hand, and use it as though it were their own, and write without perhaps controlling the mind of the person thus influenced. They take possession of the organ of speech, through which they speak, to a great extent, as they would with their own physical organization. Children are sometimes used in this way, speaking things utterly impossible for them to have conceived by their own faculties.

There are many who speak different languages, who are entirely ignorant of all but their own. The persons who control them use the language in which they spoke during their earth life; and often those who are familiar with that language converse with them in this way, the person through whom it is done being entirely ignorant of what is transpiring. I have seen two persons thus controlled by two spirits converse with each other in their own language, while neither of the persons (mediums) through whom they communicated knew anything of what they were saying.

An intimate friend of mine in Memphis, many years since, was very much opposed to these things. He said, however, if they would write through him, in a language which he did not understand, and it was ascertained that it was a language, and sensible communication, that he would believe them. They, or something, took him at his word, and for weeks and months he wrote in Hebrew, Chinese, and perhaps other languages, involuntarily. This principle is confirmed, I think, in the New Testament history. It is a law of the spiritual world, and, I think, sheds light upon every phase of these manifestations.

While I am fully convinced of the truth of the phenomena of these spiritual manifestations, and believe that the mesmeric principle explains the philosophy of them, I must repeat the caution I have so often given as to placing implicit confidence in them. Upon this principle the bad as well as the good can and do communicate; and as the evil is much more numerous in this, so it is in the other life, as to those who are in affinity with earth. Consequently, more evil and falsehood than good and truth are communicated. It is of the utmost importance for every one to bear this in mind, in order that he may be protected from all the hallucinations, visible images, involuntary writing or speaking, by which spirits would impose themselves upon him as messengers of divine truth. We were repeatedly cautioned against receiving as truth anything, no matter from what source it claimed to come, unless it was corroborated by other testimony; and to receive nothing as to doctrine that was contrary to the teachings of the Bible.

I insert two communications, purporting to have come from the father and son of an old friend. The son was killed in the battle of Chickamauga, in September, 1863. His father indulged in feelings of animosity toward the Northern people, and, from that time, they were intensified by the death of his noble boy. I have no doubt that the communications are from the relatives of my friend. I know the pure, simple, honest medium through whom they were received. She is incapable of deception. She knows nothing of Spiritualism, as it is understood; never had anything to do with "circles" or "seances;" but, in the quietude of her own room, she is controlled to write some remarkable communications, of which she knows nothing while they are being written. These communications have had a most salutary influence on the person to whom they are addressed. He has been enabled to cast out the unclean spirit of revenge by which he had been controlled, and from which he has suffered so much unhappiness. It has brought that to his mind and heart which is above all price, and he is now consecrating his heart and life to the cause to which he dedicated his young heart in youth and ripened manhood. I will not—I dare not—scoff at or ridicule such things, but hail them as great auxiliaries to draw me nearer to God, and to seek more of that purity of heart without which no one can be happy here or in the eternal world.

On November 12, 1871, he received the following:

"My Dear Father: You are waiting for my fourth epistle. You have been trying to compose your thoughts into channels of peace, but have, so far, fallen short of the true condition. I can not, with the frankness that is consistent with truth, congratulate your success. Imperfections belong not to spiritual victory. Such things may do about your common life; but, when it comes to matters of the soul, a total abnegation must be sealed before validity is acknowledged here. If I were pleading my cause as an advocate in the courts where human power decides,

I would contend, with firm earnestness, for what I felt my claim. I stand here an advocate, not where science is joined with justice, as measured by human thought, but as a firm but just defender of my father's will, deciding a case of great importance for courts where human skill can never reach. I stand here, in all the glory of my commission, to save a soul from its own error, to cleanse a life from all imperfect touch in the eyes of that Judge who stands supreme. I stand as an advocate of God, crowned with the power of that helmet and shield, with no petty fee in promise, but feelings of great pride, in a cause so noble and just. I told you I am happy, and what you must do to gain your peace, but I see little change. You sometimes imagine you have changed, but I see down to the base of this ill-fated structure. I would not speak as I feel I must, but I find the case demands the act. I am grieved to draw the mantle from so foul a corpse as I see buried in your breast—a foul corruption of hidden form you can not see.

"My dear father, what may I offer to crave your pardon for what I must subscribe to, in order to give you a faithful picture of all this? Comfort him, oh, angels of the blessed! for I, his son, in whom he sees no flaw, must draw this mantle from a form so hideous in the sight of my King! But I must take my stand before the lawful court as his accuser. Oh, faithful friends of many happy times, come, bind the draperies gently over the bleeding form! When it becomes the part of an advocate to argue in the court of Christ, it is that champion's duty to speak plainly all the cause. I here avow myself the defendant in my father's name. You stand accused of high treason, charged against you in the Book of Doom. In the first place, your faults are many. Before the hour I sealed, with my blood, my devotion to my country's pride and honor you did not yield with submission, as you should, to the chances of war. When the solemn words reached you that I was no more, instead of bowing meekly to that issue, you raised a hell of bitter feeling in your hitherto manly breast, and, with the fury of undying hate, fed the flames that have raised a volcano of such magnitude against you that was never yet reached in human mind. You took my distorted image, as you fancied my appearance, moldering in an unknown and unlettered tomb, drawing all the wrappings of funeral despair around, what seemed to friends, the fate of war.

"I stand here to expose your faults; not to worry, but to convince. You have hugged this foul compound for long years. I take this last opportunity I shall claim again for an indefinite period, so I will say all. You have dragged this dreadful carcass around with you for long years, so, of course, it is hard to eradicate what has become second nature. I see it, as it is, with no cover. You still hold the skeleton, where you seem to inspect it at will, which you do often, to my great dissatisfaction. I am your friend, when I tell you it is not gone—only smothered a little; indeed, so little, it is very hard to see any difference. You fool credulity when you say 'I am all right.' I tell you, my dear father, I know best. You are not as well by far as I wish you to be, for you lay this corpse out often in your mind, fix it up with corresponding gloom, hold it in state in the secret chambers of your soul, but draw a white, filmy shade over its huge ugliness, thinking this is sufficient, leaving the rest to the future.

"I am not content with this. I must have all to carry to my King, or I must plead again. What do you offer me, when I tell you I must work till I can wipe this blot from the page of doom? What can I do, unless you coincide with me? I have prayed, watched, worked, and fought with you, but you desert me ever in the fight. I am almost discouraged to proceed. I want my courage brightened sometimes. I can only receive it from you. I have much to battle for. I am your advocate where your voice reaches but imperfectly. I am your counsel where no one else could touch your need. This you admit. I am your defender when fresh causes come to blot your hope when all is known. I have made every testimony of my case known to you as well as I can; but still you hold aloof.

"My dear father, why do you treat me thus? I thought you loved me beyond all chance; still you leave to chance the boon I have asked as my reward. Wherefore need I plead but for you? I am happy—blessed! I have no boon to ask in my own good, for I have all God can give; I only plead for you. If I fail in eloquence, you, in your wisdom, deem so requisite, why, my dear father, please substitute my great love in the absence of all this. If I fail in any point I might make more plain, why leave that to my ignorance, but, oh, never to the cause I plead! I am pure; so pure, I am neither part nor particle of any fraud, or seeming fraud; therefore what I speak is holy, as the great cause is just. Oh, my father, put this shadow forever from thy life! I have brought all the ways I could to bear on this subject. If I could only see you forgiven, I would fly to you on the wings of speed to warn you of this great joy; but still when I kneel at the great white throne the answer is, 'Nay.' I wait and plead, but still the sound rolls through the archives of eternity's long echoes, ' No, no; never till he is pure!' What proof is this, my noble father, that you are changed? Can you blame me when I still entreat, and, when entreaty fails, that I should then demand? I am your soul's great pacifier; therefore I take no counterfeit in the way I claim. I must bring my trust in all that is beyond the slightest taint before I can give my sanction. You do not promise, only with your lips. I must have spirit proof before I can accept.

How long must I wander on the boundary of your darksome valley before I shall take the offering so acceptable to God? How long must my spirit wail out for thee without reward? I gained the privilege to go to you, and, when this was granted, I found the means to make myself known to you through this spirit friend. I came, controlling my desire to avoid the haunts of sin, to bring you this peace. Still, oh that I must still be so sad to know this thought, this fact, I may not carry to my God the proof of your reform. No, my dear father, you are not changed—only tempt your own cunning when you suppose so. Oh, how many on earth are guilty of this fraud! It is not enough to think, but you must have proof, before it avails one jot with God. Such changes only delude, instead of blessing the one in fault. I can not be your friend unless you accept what I offer. You must give up this sin; it is a sin of dark cast. You sometimes say you will do all you can to live up to my desire. When you speak thus I am both glad and pained, for I still claim my proof. When you deny all your good words by going down and gathering up the old shapes, covering them anew, till you get the whole monster where it was before, and I come with troops of angels to draw oblivion over a form so sad; but still your spirit calls it back, setting it full in view, till spirits even weep to see one so bent on his own loss. What is there so pleasing in a spectacle so unfair, to give such grim food for constant thought? I think other reflections would suit one of your refined taste much better. I want to understand the secret I have so far failed to solve.

"I am weary of this trial, if it must only end forever in such failure. I love you so fondly, it draws my deepest condemnation on your head when I have always to return with my old petition still, only yet to hear the tolling sound of the death-knell reverberated along the measureless realms of space. Oh, when will all this cease? I know you can do what I ask, but when will it be fulfilled? Oh, my dear father! I appeal to all your noble mind, to every high-born trait; I ask in the name of my God, whom you perjure by your ill-kept vows. Remember when you pray, "Forgive me as I forgive," how ill you keep your part. I beg, of all your hopes both on earth and here, to root this evil from your soul. You are not conscious of its huge deformity.

"Now, I could have written a much more beautiful letter, but I am at the substance, not gilding. We must have a firm bottom, or the structure will topple for the want of strength. I appeal to you, by all the love you bear my name, by the sins you have offered in memory to me, to blot out this dark sin forever. I beg you to do this for my sake. Do not feel worried, when you can look this change, in your honest way, straight in the face, and say with your spirit, I forgive them. Then can I go with all this joy to God, and the loud hosannahs will be shouted through all the heavenly choir; and I will fold my spirit's shield in peace about your life, scaling its close in the peaceful garb of love; and the last sleep will come as sweetly as the purest joy of Psalmist's tenderest chord when notes of harmony accord."

On November, 21, 1871, he received the following:

"MY DEAR SON—You have often wished for my presence, or some sign of my presence. Your mother is your shield, I have other interests to attend to; I have general watch to keep over my flock. This is a beautiful system, son, that we still keep the right before our children, even when they no longer see us. I am always busy, first with one, then with another, trying to settle their course through channels of duty and Godlike peace; but you are so well provided for, I never made special application to offer my remarks. We entreat before we can accomplish our desires, even in the smallest way; so you must not think it strange or feel hurt when friends don't answer your curious wish. Spirits are not creatures of will, but powers subservient to God's command. Do not feel badly if I should not come again; and never ask for what is unnecessary, for it costs us a great deal of severe prayer to gain your idle behests. I am perfectly blessed. Serve God, my son, in every act of your life; this is the one great principle of creation. If the vast world accepted its legitimate ruler, it would be a great garden of love and peace, instead of a fratricidal field. You think of going into the service of the ministry. You think well, my son, if you feel pure in the purpose—I mean if you can prove that you are indeed pure. There is a great difference between thinking, and being so. I will give you the test: Whenever you can meet every exigency of life with composure, yielding all to God's disposal, with cheerful spirit, reserving nothing, then you may feel humbly secure. My son, you can never feel humble enough, for man, however good, is indeed a mere nothing compared with God; still, the nature he has given makes both collectively united. The thought, the substance of the soul, is ever existent, and makes its own merit as it is used; therefore, son, try always to make that link pure in the strength of its perfection. You have been ably corrected in the principal fault of your life. Tom is a noble boy still, with far more fame in the Volume of God than you could gather for him in either Church or state, college or university; and as the cause of your great transgression has been the main cause of having it removed, you must not feel secure to settle down in contentment with this for your warrant: that you no longer sin in this way; but you must try to have the old fault less, by the character you apply to men who sin like you— in every action of your life. Remember, pure water flows from crystal fountains only, not from muddy gorges; so, if you hope to impress others, you must be genuinely impressed yourself. Tell Anthony, when he comes, that I left a message for him, which is my blessing. I would like to offer the same compliment to my grandson, sending him forth to battle in the army of Christ, with a fervent Godspeed; but he would not acknowedge its worth; so I will not intrude, but leave it in substance, if not in expression. I bless all my children, praying as they need, but stay not particularly with; any for work of this nature belongs to me. What a great privilege, son, for a parent to shelter his fold even when the river is between. You are as happy, I know, as you can be, under existing circumstances. I would advise you to settle your mind by engaging in some definate occupation. I believe you are not equal to the task of carrying on your farm pecuniarily, as well as lacking in labor. I would much prefer your remaining in the cottage, as you are domestically, for mother is most pleased with this home; she is standing by me now, and says, 'tell Finnie not to forget the tree, and to fix it where we can both enjoy its shade when it is hot; and when we read it will make sweet symphony with beautiful thoughts when the summer breeze plays with its foliage.' I like to please her, for she was my comfort and my help in life's trying strife, and to her lofty character do I owe much of my present happiness and distinction. Tell my darling daughter, your precious wife, that she has my double benediction; for her pure and lofty character, and her sublime faith in God have helped you to lift your steps above the quagmire of hate. I bless you jointly, and all my earthly representatives also. Be true to your God and all that it involves, before either success or peace will open before your wandering exile in the flesh. I have written you a long letter, and have intended doing it long, but for many general delays, have found this my first opportunity.

"I shall not write again, may be never. You know your

duty, and have many to still point the way. I may not have permission to come soon, so God bless you, my child, and come to your father in the land of joy and rest, earned by your love and duty in the service of God."

His father died in 1863, aged ninety-two years. For nearly fifty years he was a class-leader in the Methodist Church, and a recording steward of the circuit.

This, like many other things God has bestowed upon us, may be a blessing or a curse. If we blindly receive everything as truth coming from spirits, we will soon be out at sea without chart, rudder, or compass, and our ship will soon be wrecked in the whirlpool of error. Fire left alone in its fury is a destroying element; cared for and governed is a most valuable servant of man, performing the most important work in developing the resources of our country. We are borne over the ocean in the floating palace by water and fire, yet the one will burn, the other drown you. So with spiritual intercourse. Governed and directed wisely it is a great blessing; misguided it may do much mischief. Hence I have advised some to have nothing to do with it, because I believed they would be absorbed by it, so as to disqualify them for the duties of life. I have advised another class to investigate it. The atheist, the materialist I have thought would be greatly benefited, and could not be injured by it. When its true character is properly understood, its potency to evil will be greatly reduced, if not entirely destroyed.

One of the very first lessons we must learn is, that for awhile we are precisely the same beings we were before we passed over the river called Death. Yet there are many who will not stop to learn this lesson. They imagine because they are spirits that they know a great deal more. We must bear in mind that we are spirits now as much as we will be then. Our surroundings only will be different. We are liable to err there as well as here. We must not be led away by the fascination of the intercourse to overlook this important question. From what kind or condition does this intelligence come? Is it from a human being like yourself?—one liable to be mistaken, be he ever so honest in his convictions of the truth of what he may be saying, to say nothing now of the innumerable number of lying, deceiving spirits who can communicate as well as the truthful? There was no truth more earnestly and frequently mentioned than this in our investigations. "Our intercourse is not, can not be perfect." It does not, can not speak with authority, and in everything communicated we must use our own judgment.

What shall we do with it? It is springing up in all parts of the earth, and leading millions into captivity. Is there no medium for us between blind faith, in its teachings and knowledge, between fanaticism and infidelity, between superstition and reason? Can we, amid this deluge of time, find no Ararat on which our ark may rest, and whence we may send our dove to return with its olive-branch, rather than the raven to perish amid the desert waste of waters? Let us, however, bear in mind that amid all the discouragements, difficulties and errors that attend our researches the truth can be found by the persevering investigator. Truth and error are in mortal life ever mingled together, and it is the part of wisdom to separate them, and not reject the truth because error sits down beside it and assumes its guise.

The man of science calls it superstition; the man of the world calls it delusion; many of the religionists characterize it as satanic. In either case it is well worthy the investigation of the learned, rather than their scoffs and sneers. If faith can be placed in human testimony then these manifestations are as well established as any other facts can be which depend upon evidence. Every avenue through which we gain information is used in demonstrating, beyond the possibility of doubt, to the honest inquirer, the truth of these manifestations.

I copy from Hon. Robert Dale Owens' "Debatable Land" what was the result of his experience relative to these teachings, stating here, as I have often done, that for even a longer time of examination my experience and observation has been identical with his upon this subject. He says, addressing the Protestant clergy: "Many of your number are probably deterred from entering upon this task by the idea that the alleged phase of modern revelation is anti-Christian in tendency. If, after a varied experience of sixteen years in different countries, I am entitled to offer an opinion, it is that if such spiritual communications be sought in an earnest, becoming spirit, the views presented will, in the vast majority of cases, be in strict accordance with the teachings of Christ, such as we may reasonably conceive these to have been from the testimony of his evangelical biographers—the breath, the very essence of his divine philosophy. The following may be taken as the great leading principles on which intelligent Spiritualists unite:

"1. This is a world governed by a God of love and mercy, in which all things work together for good to those who reverently conform to his eternal laws.

"2. In strictness there is no death. Life continues from the life which now is into that which is to come. In all cases in which life is well spent the change which men are wont to call death is God's last and best gift to his creatures here.

"3. The earth phase of life is an essential preparation for the life which is to come. Its appropriate duties and callings can not be neglected without injury to human welfare and development both in this world and the next. Even its enjoyments, temperately accepted, are fit preludes to the happiness of a higher state.

"4. The phase of life which follows the death change is in strictest sense the supplement of that which precedes it. . . . Vastly wiser and more dispassionate than we, they are still, however, fallible, and they are governed by the same general laws of being modified only by corporeal disenthralment to which they were subjected here.

"5. Our state here determines our initial state there. In the next world we simply gravitate to the position for which by life on earth we fitted ourselves. There is no instantaneous change of character when we pass the present phase of life. Our virtues, our vices, our intelligence, our ignorance, all pass over with us, modified, doubtless, but to what extent we know not, when the spiritual body emerges divested of its fleshly incumbrance, yet essentially the same as when the death slumber came over us.

"The sufferings there are natural sequents of evil doing and evil thinking here; are as various in character and in degree as the enjoyments, but they are mental, not bodily. There have always existed intermundane laws according to which men may occasionally obtain, under certain conditions, revealings from those who have passed to the next world before them. A certain proportion of human beings are more sensitive to spiritual perceptions than their fellows; and it is usually in their presence, or through the medium of one or more, that ultramundane intercourse occurs. When the conditions are favorable, and the sensitive, through whom the manifestations come, is highly gifted, these may supply important materials for thought, and valuable rules of conduct. But the spiritual phenomena, in their highest phases, do much more than this. They furnish proof addressed to the reason and tangible to the senses, of the reality of another life, better and happier than this, and of which our earthly pilgrimage is but the novitiate. They bring immortality to light under a blaze of evidence which outshines, as the sun the stars, all traditional or historical testimonies. For surmise they give us conviction, and assured knowledge for wavering belief. In all this there is no speculative divinity. Further than this, I have never, out of thousands of communications, received one that denounced any sincere religious opinion, whether Catholic or Protestant, Mahommedan or Hindoo. . . .

"Does it occur to you that modern spiritual phenomena, which men so able and so little disposed to superstition admit as realities, may be worth looking into? Hundreds of thousands feel assured to-day that they have this clear and irresistible evidence for immortality. Think of such a living conviction. Consider how it stands out above all that wealth or fame and every earthly good fortune can bestow—the blessing of blessings, which the world can neither give nor take away."

I have no comments to make on these things, but leave every one to draw their own inferences, which, doubtless, will be in accordance with their opinion of these things. They certainly are of such a character as to deserve an investigation by those who desire to know the truth. We can not ignore the facts. We can not believe that the millions who believe in them are deceived. Having for near a score of years believed them, I have pursued the even tenor of my way, in the discharge of the duties assigned me by the Church, paying little or no attention to the subject since our investigations closed, in 1855.

The subject of "the old clock striking," and the manner in which I was treated by the St. Louis *Christian Advocate*, has been the occasion of bringing before the public the contents of this book. Whatever of good or evil it may produce may be, in part at least, attributed to the "clock story," and the manner of its discussion.

The spirit of free inquiry is abroad in the world. There is special earnestness manifested in a critical analysis of the Bible and its claims to supernatural origin. The open atheist, who scoffs at mystery and miracles, and professes to believe nothing that he can not analyze, is puzzled at these manifestations. Skepticism arising from the general stimulus of thought is not so formidable an enemy of the Christian religion as many suppose. It is a salutary phase of the ordinary evolution of the mind. By detecting and exposing error, it prepares the way for the advent of truth. Powerful and aggressive as it is, I think its mission is drawing to a close. The means are already being prepared by which the human mind, however cultivated and scientific, shall be elevated to a higher and purer light than has ever been shed upon it. Difficulties which have been considered insurmountable will be removed, obscurities will be explained and reconciled, the skeptic silenced, and the Christian enlightened, when revelation is seen as a perfected whole. Divine truth shall burst forth with new glory from the spiritual sense of the *holy Word of God*. The Church has executed its commission according to the letter of that word. Its tendency however, has been to formalism. Not only the Romish, but the Protestant Churches, have trusted too much in the imposing forms and ceremonies of their religious worship. The human mind has arrived at that stage of progression when it bursts the bonds of literal or sensuous interpretation of the Word of Life. There are aspirations for that which is above the old methods of interpretation, which were necessary in former times. This inevitable warfare between the spirit and the letter will cease only with a complete victory of the former. "The letter killeth, but the spirit giveth life." In its triumphs it will enlighten, revive, purify, and bless the Church by light from heaven. There will be no new revelation, but the opening of the seals which have hidden from our eyes the spiritual sense of the Word of God.

The credibility of the Christian religion depends greatly upon the universality of the laws and principles upon which it is founded. What was done two or four thousand years ago, under similar conditions can be done now. If we believe that Jacob, Moses, Ezekiel, or John had visions of angels, we must admit it to be possible for persons to have similar visions in the present age. If Paul was carried up to the third heaven while still living in the body, why may not others thus have their spiritual eyes opened to see the paradise of God? These things, I think, are being repeated, with the necessary modifications, beneath the critical eyes of philosophy and science.

If the theology and psychology of the Bible are true, of which we have not the slightest doubt, then these things, stupendous as they may at first seem, are not only practicable and credible, but irresistible. The sincere Christian should hail them with joy as the time spoken of by our Lord, when we should see the angels of God ascending and descending. Revelation has its successive steps and degrees, one unfolding out of and founded upon the other. Theology, when properly understood, and science are both from God. Hence, there can be no conflict, the one with the other. It is ignorance of one or the other which makes some believe there is antagonism between them. There is really no mystery, but ignorance. The vast volume of nature, spread out before us, when properly understood, and the revelations God has made in his Word, harmonize with each other. Science and true theology are married. The truths of each are written upon their face, to those who have discernment enough to discover them. "He that hath ears to hear, let him hear." He that hath eyes to see, let him see what is now being effected by the instrumentalities of these manifestations. It is only from a spiritual stand-point that we are prepared to understand and appreciate these heavenly truths, which are in harmony with the same truths and principles recorded in the Bible.

Having now given my honest views of what I believe to be the truth, I wish it to be distinctly understood that I represent no one but myself. No sect, party, or Church is in any sense responsible for what I have written. Not that I claim to be the author, but the amanuensis of what I have received, mainly through the teachings at our circle. I have been to no other. I have copied, from various sources, what I believed to be the truth, which is in harmony therewith. Sometimes I have quoted without giving the author of the sentiment expressed. The book, such as it is, has been written amid a pressure of other duties, without time to rewrite and correct, as I desired to have done. I know it has many imperfections. I make no claim to originality as to the truths contained, or the manner in which they are expressed. I have done what I felt it my duty to perform, leaving the result with Him who can bring order out of confusion, harmony out of chaos, and make even the weak things confound the mighty.

I ask an unprejudiced verdict from those who have followed me through these pages, as to whether the facts contained therein be not in accordance with the Scriptures of Divine Truth.

Joshua Soul

O Try Wm R Roston

Mallie. Levin Watson

Stephen Olin,

Moses Brack

Saml Elbert

Wm Hyer

Mary A Tate

John Newland Muffett

Susannah Morgan

J W Andrew

Chas Scott

CHAPTER XIV.

COMMUNICATIONS RECEIVED THROUGH DR. J. V. MANSFIELD, 361 SIXTH AVENUE, NEW YORK.

On the 22d day of May Rev. Philip Tuggle, Presiding Elder of the Holly Springs District, North Mississippi Conference, and myself called on Dr. M. to deliver a letter from a friend in Memphis to him.

He met us at the door and invited us up-stairs.

"We have come," said I, "to deliver this letter, and expose, if we can, what you profess to do."

He, smiling, taking each one of us by the hand, said: "I will take this one first."

Brother Tuggle wrote, asking if there was any one present who wished to communicate with him?

One was written signed, Minerva Scruggs. Brother T. did not seem to recognize the name; when it was written I was the wife of Phineas T. Scruggs. In it she expressed her joy that he had come there with me. The Doctor turned to me while reading it, and asked me if my name was Watson? He then wrote as follows:

"Bless you, bless my dear son, for the assurance I have you allow me a place in your heart of hearts. Your precious, dear mother, Susannah, and I, together with your friend Andrews, have been with you for years—yes, as you have traveled up and down the earth cogitating in your mind what was duty. Often would you ask yourself, 'If a man die shall he live again?' With all your faith in the Book of books, of the soul's immortality you have at times doubted; or wondered, if you might not be mistaken. Then, at times, you have said in your soul, as you talked to the multitude, that you could not be mistaken;

and you have declared your faith in the revelation of the Bible. In this way you have lived until you heard those tiny raps, and other maifestations, which satisfied your mind they originated from an intelligence beyond. You have, from time to time, made records of such manifestations, and, after looking them over and over, you have thought, and that wisely too, to put them into book form. The work is one that will do an immense good. But of that I will say more by and by. Your old friend Samuel Gilbert and Calvin W. Cherry are with me now, and bid me say to you, Dare to be bold in the defence of truth that wells up in your soul from day to day. You ought to be thankful—I know you are—that you have lived to see this light within your soul. Go on, my son; mind not what the would-be wise may say or think. Know you are in talking distance with your dear departed,

"Your father, LEVIN WATSON."

(My father was a Methodist from his youth. I think he was a class-leader about forty years of his life.)

Soon after this it was written:

"Can I see you, dear Brother Watson, where I can talk with you, where I can thank you for your good feelings toward me in life. Again, even in death, you did not forget to speak kindly of me. I was by many thought to be a religious fanatic; but, Brother Watson, my faith in that Book, which you know was my meat and drink for years, arried me safe over the Jordan of life, as it has millions of millions before me. I acted, or endeavored to act, up to its precepts, and in doing so I was happy. I had often heard of the new ism, and the new ship, but I thought best to stick to the old ship, knowing that was sure. But, brother, I now see how vastly more good I could have done on earth, or to my fellow-mortals, had the light of spirit communion lit up my heart and mind, as it has yours. Brother, you need not be ashamed to speak out boldly, in your valuable paper, or book, of the truth of spirit communion. The time is fast approaching when it will swallow up all other isms, and there will be one universal Church or brotherhood, instead of the many taught even at your time of life.

"Your forthcoming book will be criticised by the Church; but care not for that, it is a step in the right direction. But of that I will say more hereafter. You would ask me if I found the spirit world as I had anticipated? Oh, Brother, let me assure you it far surpasses anything I had ever hoped of enjoying. While on earth my theme was the Hill of Calvary; here it is PROGRESSION, upward and onward forever.

"Will you say to the dear ones in Augusta that Brother Andrews is often with them, and would talk with them.

"Your brother, J. D. ANDREWS."

"FRIEND WATSON: Tell Dixon we shall meet again. . . . Could you have witnessed the meeting of friend Poston and daughter, as I did. They called me Judge.

"CHARLES SCOTT."

On the 24th I called again on Dr. Mansfield, and wrote privately, asking if my wife would communicate with me, wrapping it up in several folds of paper. It was then written:

"Do not scold me, Brother, for taking time you intended your once precious consort should have improved, but she is not present this moment. I have thought I would finish my communication given you the other day, which I failed to do for want of control. You wanted me to give the places included in my circuits in Arkansas. Well: *Dardanelle, Dover, Clarksville, Augusta,* and *Richland, Jackson Co.* I died about thirteen miles from Augusta, in Jackson Co., December 3d, 1859, full in the hope of a glorious immortality. Thank God! I was not disappointed· only happily so. Be firm, Brother

Watson, look aloft, and see the signs of the times in golden letters.

"Your brother, J. D. ANDREWS."

It was then written:

"Oh my dear, dear, ever kind and loving husband! have you thought of your dear Mary; do you often think of the happy days while we were permitted each other's society? As to me, those were numbered among my happiest on earth. And did I not know, Samuel, we should meet again, and that to never again be dissevered, then I would be wretched indeed; but knowing all shall meet, and know we love as we loved on earth, my cup of bliss is full.

"Do not weep, Samuel, but shout aloud for joy at the prospect before you. You are doing your work, and doing it well, too. Be not ashamed to declare your faith in spirit communion; for the time is not far distant when this great light of spirit intercommunion shall displace all lesser lights, and all SHALL see as one. You will be blessed in the publication of your new work, although it meet with severe criticism; yet, Samuel, fear not, it is truth; it will stand the test of criticisms, be they whatever they may.

"I would be pleased to tell you more about my beautiful home, but as you want to talk with others, perhaps I had better defer it until another time. Samuel, bless you! Bless you, for this call! Go where you may, I will go with you; and when you are to cross the river that divides time and eternity listen, and you shall hear the splash of the boatman's oar. Then know that your Mary is near you. Love to all the dear ones at home, and believe me, as ever,

"Your wife, MOLLIE."

I then wrote, and folded privately, the name of my old friend Wm. K. Poston. This is what was written:

"BROTHER WATSON: This is more than I had anticipated or hoped for, and you may say more than I really deserved for my stubbornness to investigate the subject about which you and I had much conversation. Well, very well, do I recollect of talking with you and Brother Williams time and again on the subject of spirit communion, and at times might have uttered sentences that were calculated to wound your generous and truthful feelings; but, Brother Watson, I believed all you said came from an honest heart, yet to me, it appeared, the subject was ridiculous. The idea that you could talk with your dear loved ones departed, and I could not get a word from my darling daughter, or others of my dear ones departed, was to me an idea preposterous.

"But ah, Brother Watson, we know not what a day or an hour may bring forth. One hour after I had awaked to consciousness in the spirit land, I would have been willing to have given all the treasures of earth, were they mine, could I have but returned to you and begged your pardon for my manner of reasoning with you and Brother Gilbert; but that was denied me. Again I say, as I did once in Memphis to you, 'Spiritualism is true, and so is the Bible.' Wesley was right. Brother Watson, let me abjure you to let your light shine while you tarry in the body. Cry aloud, and spare not!

"WM. K. POSTON."

A few words of explanation are necessary to understand the above communication. The writer and myself had been intimately associated since 1838, in Clarksville, Tenn. He was one of the first who professed religion and joined the Church after I went to that station. He came to Memphis soon after I did, in the fall of 1839. Few men have been more intimately associated than we were for more than a quarter of a century. We lived near each other, at Greenwood. Our families were upon terms of great intimacy.

On the subject of spirit communion he was the worst

case I ever saw. He honestly believed that there was a conflict between that and the Bible. This formed the basis of his unconquerable prejudice against the whole subject. He has told me that, while he had the utmost confidence in what I said about it—that I was honest—yet he would not believe it, if a thousand of the best and most truthful men would declare it.

He was one of the most prominent lawyers of the city, for many years one of the best class-leaders I ever saw, and wielded as much influence in the Church and community as any man that I have ever known in it.

There is one sentence in his communications which deserves notice and explanation—"Spiritualism is true, and so is the Bible." I was passing along Second Street one day last summer, when a friend called me to his office. He was one of those I have mentioned as talking to and seeing spirits. A niece of his, who died a few months previous, was with him most of the time. He said that she wanted to talk to me; that she always had loved me, but that she loved me more since she had gone to the spirit land, than she ever did before. Among other things, I asked her if she saw Mr. Poston. She replied, "Yes, every day." "Can you get him to come here?" "Yes, in a few minutes." Soon the gentleman said, "Poston says he wants to shake hands with you." Said I, "Poston, you know we often talked of this subject while you were here. What do you think of it now?" He replied, "I have changed my opinion entirely in regard to it. Spiritualism is true, and so is the Bible."

I had kept this matter to myself; but now I feel it due to truth to mention it, as it was to my mind, if I had needed it, a good test of the truth of these things. I then wrote for Rev. Wm. McMahon, when this response was written:

"DEAR MR. WATSON: You may think it singular in this,

my seeming intrusion, coming not only unsolicited, but taking time you had hoped might have been occupied by your friend McMahon. But as your friend was not present, Major Winchester and Dr. Gilbert and Lycurgus Gabbert, M.D., thought I might improve the time without being considered an intruder. Well, very well do I remember you, and your ministrations with the people of Memphis—at an early day, when I was acting as amanuensis for the inhabitants of the spirit world, to this dear people. But as well do I recollect the prejudice, the bitter feeling manifested toward me, not because I had a drop of dark or African blood in my veins, but that I had once been the wife of Colonel Winchester, who had, at an early day, married a wife who, as the Memphis people would, and often did say, was a 'little off color.' But a kinder, nobler-hearted woman never lived than the mother of his now living daughters, who, by the way, are wrongfully defrauded of their rights. But of this I will say no more.

"You have taken a step that you will never regret on earth nor in heaven. I have met Mrs. Watson, Mrs. Scruggs, Mrs. Underwood, Dr. Samuel Gilbert and his son, Porter Gilbert, Mrs. Leatherman, Gen. Thomas Rivers, Mr. Cherry, Judge Scott, Mr. Davis, Ignatius A. Spaulding, and others I could mention, had I time.

"Go on with your book. Dare to speak out the full gushings of your heart. God and his angels will shield you against all attacks. If I have done wrong in taking this time, so precious, pardon, pardon.

"LUCY LEONORA WINCHESTER."

To the old citizens of Memphis this communication has several strong tests. It is a truthful history of those times. The last name I never heard of that I remember. I read it to Major M. J. Wicks, Col. Sam Tate, and W. B. Greenlaw, in their room, at the St. Nicholas Hotel, the same evening. The two latter knew him well. Col. Tate said the first stage he ever saw was owned by him. This lady I knew during her former husband's life, while a widow, and as the wife of Major Winchester, one of the first settlers, and most influential men of Memphis. She is the lady to whom I refer of a citizen of Memphis speaking through her of his hypocrisy.

Next day I wrote for my wife, to tell me of her parents and our children; when it was written:

"Bless you, darling one, for this, another call. I have been with you much since my talk with you yesterday. Yes, Samuel, I have impressed you with my nearness. Your mind has scarcely been alive to anything else since our talk yesterday. You would read, or attempt to read, your proof; but you would find yourself or mind wandering away to your dear Mollie. You ask me as to my dear parents. Well, I am with them often; also our darling ones who are dwellers of the land of souls. But, Samuel, as our spheres are not the same, please call each separately, and allow them to talk with you. We have messengers that belong to the several spheres, whose business it is to call them that are by our friends related. Yes, Samuel, I meet them often. Those that are in more advanced conditions or spheres return to those who inhabit lower spheres, and thus we encourage each other, onward and upward, in the race of endless progression. Samuel, my dear one, be of good cheer; the angels are with you; you need have no fear for the future.

"Lovingly, your spirit wife, MOLLIE.
"*May* 25, 1872."

I then wrote for my eldest daughter, Bettie; when was written:

"MY DEAR FATHER—My soul more than rejoices at this opportunity of talking with you, separated as we are. My mother told me of her interview with you yesterday, and since that time my soul has been frantic to speak with you. And yet, dear father, I came tremblingly this morning, for fear you would not find time to allow me even a few words. I was called by that sweet young lady spirit, Virginia Dixon, who is in my sphere. She said, 'Bettie, do not fear; we can and will overcome all obstacles, and you shall talk with your dear Pa.' Well, here I am, and so happy to *know*. I have if but a feeble control to speak with you, my dear pa. Mother dear is more than happy to know she has reached you, and that to your mind so satisfactory. She is not willing to leave you day or night. Well, father, I have duties that call me away now, but will return to you again, and tell you more of my dear home. So, for awhile, adieu. Your BETTIE."

I then wrote for my eldest son, Allen.

"Oh, my dear, dear father, this is more than I have hoped for—at least at this sitting. Dear Judge Poston sent a messenger for me saying, 'Allen, my dear young friend, do, do hasten and talk with your dear father, who is just outside awaiting you.' At this summons my soul shouted glory to God in the highest! Well, dear father, is this not blessed? Does not this remove every doubt of the soul's immortality being a truth? Yes, yes, father. You know my darling sisters and mother live, and because they do, you will also. Mother is preparing you a bower beside her, and we are, one and all, weaving evergreens and rose-vines over and about it, that you may know when you come here we have had pleasant thoughts of a husband and father.

"Well, father, go on in your labor of love, for the people you once called to associate with you are leaving tracks that time can not obliterate. As mother said, you are doing your work, and doing it well, too.

"I would not be selfish and take more time, for others would speak with you.

"Your affectionate son, ALLEN."

I then wrote for Bishop Otey; when it was written:

"DEAR BRO. WATSON—Your dear friend, the Bishop, is not at present with you; but Stephen Olin is, and he says your book will be a success. He has been with you while you have been weaving it, and so has Mr. Wesley. They say the book will not only produce a sensation, but great good will result from the wide-spread of the truths therein contained. I have not looked it over, nor was there need of it so long as those two God-gifted spirits have had the management of it.

"Very truly, JOHN NEWLAND MAFFITT.
"*May 25, '72.*"

I then asked for Bishop Soule's opinion of it.

"DEAR BRO.—If my judgment on the matter of your book is worth seeking, allow me to say it will be to the conscientious and thirsty soul for more light, apples of gold in trays of silver. Bro. Taylor told me he believed the book would be the medium through which the South and the North would be again united. Well, Bro., time works wonders. You are in safe hands and keeping.

"Your brother, JOSHUA SOUL.
"To Samuel Watson.
"*May 25, '72.*"

I then wrote for Gen. Thomas Rivers, when was written:

"How can I sufficiently thank you, yea, bless you, for this assurance I have you yet allow me a place in your heart-memory? When my sister Minerva, who was the wife of Judge Phineas T. Scruggs, came for me, said Bro. Tom, 'Do you know that your friend, Bro. Watson, is seeking an interview with you?' At this my soul became frantic, for the news was too good to be believed. However, by the assistance of B. R. Webb, who, you well recollect, was shot by T. B. Minot on Main Street, in your city, came, and said, 'General, allow me to assist you in this control.' Then came Dr. Gilbert and W. B. Rose, who was killed in the Confederate army, and through their united control I am assisted to write.

"Well, Bro., what shall I say about that which has already been spoken. You have no prejudices or doubts to combat. The highway that leads from earth to the spirit land is clear before you; for at times Dr. Gilbert and Rainford Brownelly say you have a sight of the promised land, or, in other words, you are nearly on the top round of the ladder. One step more, and you step into the land that 'flows with milk and honey.' You have nothing to fear, but much to gain.

"I have met my dear parents, brothers, and sisters, my two darling wives, and have prepared a mansion large for my now earth wife, Lucetta, who will come to be with me when her mission on earth is finished. Well, Bro., I found the spirit land much as you and I had conjectured it would be, only the story had not been half told us as to its reality and beauty.

"Be faithful to your light. It will light you to another ight that will not change in heaven, save to grow brighter and more beautiful to all eternity.

"When I took my breastplate and sword and walked out to defend my country, I little thought my life was to be sacrificed as it was; but the cause was a just one, and could I live my life over again on earth, I would lay it on the same altar again.

"My sister, Mrs. Scruggs, says, tell her daughter, Mollie Horton, that her darling Nina is safe and happy.

"Your old friend and brother, THOS. W. RIVERS.

"*May* 25, '72."

I then wrote for Bishop Andrew; when it was written:

"BRO.—Your friend, Bro. J. O. Andrew, is not at this moment present. He is away now on duty—usually he is with you. JOHN FRAZER.

"I was a Methodist preacher. Dr. Samuel Gilbert knew me well. J. F."

I then wrote for Rev. Moses Brock; when it was written:

"I have been standing by and witnessing others speak with you, and was led to think I was not among the favored few that was to speak with you to-day; but, in the largeness of your soul, you did embrace your old friend M. B., and my soul says, 'Thanks, thanks.' Bro., what has been told you to-day will go with you through the balance of your earth life. As your friend, the General, has told you, you have nothing to fear.

"Your old friend,   MOSES BROCK."

My time having nearly expired, I wrote for my mother; when was written:

"Who but a mother could know the joy such an interview afforded? Samuel, my dear son, I and your father, Levin, have often talked the matter of your exercises over, since we met in the spirit land. Your father says, 'Let Samuel alone. He will find in soul land by and by.' Your life has been one of investigation. Your mind, from early life, was aspiring for a something that you found not in the popular teaching of the day; so you ever taught what you believed to be the truth, let it cut where it might, and in this way of accepting the teaching of that monitor within you, which is the God part of your nature, you have been led into a light far in advance of your associated brotherhood. Continue, my son, to obey the voice within, and you will not fail to have the reward that awaits the earth-born.

"Your mother,   SUSANNAH WATSON."

Fourth interview.—Will Dr. Samuel Gilbert have Mystery, Bishop Otey, Dr. Nat. Howcott, and himself, give me their opinion of my book?

"MY DEAR BRO. WATSON—I have sent our friend

Poston to call Bishop Otey and Howcott. They will be here soon, if not otherwise engaged; but you may anticipate their views as to the book now in process of being issued. I tell you, Bro. Watson, you have done not only yourself justice, but the work you have prepared. Tell Judge Edmunds the name he gave the book is one so befitting the matter it contains.

"Ask him if he recollects me attending circles when myself, Dr. Wellington, and others, met at circle in early day. I think Dr. Alfred Hall was present. Tell the Judge his name is, to use an earth expression, a household word here. When Bro. Poston returns I will then report progress. Your friend and brother, SAMUEL GILBERT."

"Will my old schoolmate and friend, Dr. N. W. Seat, speak with me?" I asked; when was written:

"MY DEAR WATSON—Your dear Mollie anticipated your desire to call me to speak with you, having so often heard you speak of your schoolmate and friend of other early days. Well, Bro. Watson, those days, those associations, were ever to be, and ever will be, remembered by us. I can look back upon our past lives, and with pleasure recall those pleasures which we were wont to enjoy in each other's society; but those days have passed, never to be enjoyed again until we meet in the summer land, there to enjoy each other's society unbroken eternally. You have much to be thankful for, that your life was spared you to gather together all the products of your sowing, and leave it to your family and the world at large as your last will and testament. Bro., you are doing your work. Your brother, N. W. SEAT."

"DEAR WATSON—Your friend Poston calls me to you, which summons I obey with pleasure. This is kind of you to notice me and Bro. Howcott, dwelling in supernal spheres as we are. If our judgment or opinion is worth seeking, then allow us to say you never have done the world better service than in this last enterprise of yours. In a word, I will say we would not have you change one word from your present arrangement. The book has been compiled by direction of minds long since departed, and by and by you will know who they are. "OTEY.

"HOWCOTT."

"BRO. SAMUEL—How blessed is this moment to me, although I have been with you much; and often since Mollie was with me in my sphere I have visited you with her frequently. I do not pretend to say I am with you as often as Mollie is, for she is not happy unless she is with you once a day. However, Samuel, I am thankful I am permitted to come and talk with you, if but a few broken or disconnected sentences.

"I am pleased you have so much comfort from your way of communing. As to your forthcoming book, it will be all you would or can desire it.

"Your sister,   MARY."

"With pleasure, Bro. Samuel, I will speak with you. Not long since our family, those of us that have passed to the spirit land, had a family gathering, and the topic of conversation was, why should you be permitted to live and receive such light from the sphere land, while so many of the family died without the evidence you have of the soul's immortality? Mollie said, 'The good Father never makes mistakes. He trusted you with the mission because he knew you would do it justice.' Well, Brother, what Mollie says is ever to the point; so we believe all she says, as her manner of accounting for the privilege you enjoy.

"You are truly numbered among the favored few. Go on, brother, with your mission. Soon, at the furthest, you will hear the voice saying, '*Well done! Come up higher.*'

"Your brother,   WM. HENRY WATSON."

"Well, Brother, thanks be to God, our heavenly Father, you have allowed me a word with you at this time. I was not present, but was called by your sweet sister Mary, saying, 'Bro. John, hasten, hasten to speak with Bro. Samuel, for the time is limited, and perhaps he will allow you to speak after Bro. William Henry has concluded his control.'

"Here I am, Bro., and, as I said in the commencement, thanks be to God! Yes, yes, our Bro. William has truly said you are among the favored few. Bro., 'make hay, *then*, while the sun shines.' Soon it may pass into a cloud, and thus your earth vision will be obscured until you reach the land of souls. Be faithful, Bro., and know you are in special charge, and watch care of a band of spirits, who leave you not, day or night.

"Your brother,   JOHN A. WATSON."

The hour was nearly out which was engaged, when it was written:

"MY DEAR SON—As no other one seems to be present, I will improve the time—if but for a moment. Well, Samuel, it has given me as much pleasure to stand by and witness the joy at the company that has talked with you this morning as though I had talked myself. 'Truly,' say they, one and all, 'is this not blessed.'

"Well, Samuel, could you see the joy depicted in the countenance of your dear ones here at this opportunity to speak from their homes, you would say you had been well remunerated for the time you had given them. My son, allow me and your dear ones to talk with you as often as you feel you can, while you have an opportunity of so doing.

"Your mother,   SUSANNAH WATSON."

Col. Sam Tate had visited Dr. M., and asked his wife to give him the names of her associates in the spirit land, when he received the following:

"Well, darling, as to that, I have with me now Mrs.

Watson, two of Gen. Rivers' wives, the mother of your friend Dr. Williams, the wife of Judge Scruggs, and the daughter of your friend Watson—we call her here Dear Bettie. All these I found at the office of the medium, when I walked into the office with you. These are now my personal associates.

"Your wife,   MARY A. TATE."

One night after this I found the above communication in my bureau drawer. I went immediately to Major Wicks' and Col. Tate's room, and asked him to let me see the communications he got from his wife. He replied, "I tore them all up." I then produced the paper, which he said was the same he had received. He had never been in my room, nor had I ever seen the paper before. Query—How did it get there?

Fifth day.—I called on Dr. M., and asked: Will my friend W. K. Poston speak of my book?

"DEAR BROTHER WATSON—As to the forthcoming book I really do not know what more could be said that would add to the interest of that publication which engages your mind and attention at this time. You have prepared it carefully, and so have you arranged the subject-matter. It can not fail to instruct the reader, and benefit the world at large. You are an especial charge of a band of spirits who have for years been preparing your mind for this work. Be passive, and allow them to complete it; then your mission will be complete. You shall yet be called the world's benefactor.

"Your brother,   WM. K. POSTON."

I wrote the name of Rev. Wm. McMahon.

"DEAR PA—Mr. McMahon is not now present. I come to tell you the same.

"Your daughter,   BETTIE."

I then wrote the name of Bishop Andrew.

"DEAR BROTHER—Pardon the intrusion, but I come to

say your friend, the Bishop, is away at this time, and would not be able to speak to you.

     "Yours sincerely, STEPHEN OLIN."

I then wrote, Will Dr. Olin speak himself to me?

"I surely thank you, dear brother, for this condescension on your part to allow me to speak with you at this time—if but a word.

"I am not a stranger to the subject that has for years, and now does engage your whole soul. I have visited you with Coke and the Wesleys, Collingsworth, Fisk, Channing, and other leading lights, and done all we could to impress you of that which was, and now is, daily welling up in your thoughts. Oh, Brother, rejoice! shout aloud the praises of God for allowing you to be the instrument of enlightening the mind of your fellow-mortals! Can I assist you? I will do it most cheerfully.

     "Your brother, STEPHEN OLIN."

I then wrote for Rev. Wm. Hyer.

"Thanks, dear brother, for allowing me to speak with you. I had not the slightest idea you would think of me. Yet I am not less to talk with you. Truly, as it has been said to you by your friends, you are numbered among the favored ones; for while a majority of your friends, and my friends, are leaning on hope, or clinging to faith of a life beyond the grave, you can say you KNOW your dear departed live. You have tangible evidence, and knowledge admits of no faith, no doubt, but a positive reality. Go on, brother, you need not fear, the angels are with you.

     "Yours truly, WM. HYER."

I then wrote for Rev. S. G. Starks.

"DEAR BROTHER WATSON—Brother Starks is not present, or within my call. Was he, I would call him at once.

"Thank God, dear brother, you did induce my dear Adelia to come and talk with me.

     "Your brother, N. W. SEAT."

(I had called to see my old schoolmate's widow a day or two before, and suggested to her that she might hear from the doctor there.)

I then wrote, Will my dear mother speak to me, and tell me who made the clock strike "one" before each one of four of my family died?

"Well, Samuel, my son, no one in particular, but it was by the combined influence of Coke, the Wesleys, Channing, and the band that surrounded you at that time, to see what they could produce. Finding all the avenues closed to produce physical manifestations but the [here a picture of the clock was drawn by the pencil], they fell upon the machinery of the clock, and it yielded to their united efforts. Your mother, SUSANNAH."

I then wrote, Will Brother Daniel Jones speak with me?

"With all my soul, will I. Oh, bless you besides. Brother Watson, how could you think of Brother Jones, among the many you have in spirit-life to call for? Oh, Brother, this is joy beyond expression! Go on, then, in your work, enlightening the mind of your fellow-men. Your mission is a blessed one. Your reward awaits you.

"Your brother, DANIEL JONES."

This was a colored preacher, whom I had known from his boyhood. Rev. Dr. Baskerville and myself bought him. Bishop Janes was about sending him as missionary to Liberia in 1845. I visited him in his sickness. He died in Memphis many years since, sitting in his chair.

I have given the communications received through Dr. Mansfield just as they were written. The things referred to here, of which I have the information, I know to be correct. That which I did not know has been confirmed by the gentlemen from Memphis with me at the St. Nicholas Hotel. There is an error or two in regard to Christian names, but we must remember that there they do not know some things. Also that only one hour was the time allowed for, perhaps, from five to ten communications. It would be singular if they should be correct in those little matters. For instance, Gen. Rivers was mistaken in the initials of Mr. Webb, who was shot by T. B. Minott; Mrs. Winchester was mistaken in regard to Dr. Gabbert's Christian name. His father was my family physician for many years. He had three sons, all doctors. Although I have known them from their boyhood, I did not know, until Col. Sam Tate, their half-brother, told me of the error. Lycurgus is still living, and told me recently, in Memphis, that he would give twenty years hard work in his profession to know that he would live after death. There is an omission of the letter e in Bishop Soule's name. If there are any other errors in these communications, I am not aware of them. Several of them are personal, yet I have felt it due the subject to give all, just as they were written, consecutively. There are some things I was inclined to erase, as where Dr. Olin speaks of "condescension," while I felt truly I was the honored party. I never saw the Doctor, but I have always had the most profound respect for his character. There have been some strange violations of grammar and rhetoric. The use of capitals, when speaking of this book, I thought I would change, but, with this exception, I give them as received. Dr. Mansfield does not profess to give the handwriting of the individual, but there seemed so much similarity to the chirography of those with whom I had been acquainted, that I thought I would give a fac-simile of some of them. I have had put on page 180 about all it will contain of them.

Who is this medium? is a very natural inquiry. I would state that he is a man of fine moral character, who has been living in New York over thirty years, and has been class-leader long enough to have held over seventeen hundred class-meetings. I do not know that I should have gone to him, only, as mentioned, with Brother Tuggle, to deliver the letter for a friend. I had no interview with any other medium during my stay in New York. There has been no one in the room but he and myself, only the first time, as stated. I have met gentlemen and ladies there, but in another room. The Governor of the State, the editor of the *World*, and a Dr. —— were there one morning, very anxious to have an hour each. Dr. M. said that under no circumstances could he make any change; that I had engaged that time, and those who desired to communicate with me were there, and that he never yet had disappointed any one.

The manner of proceeding is this: I write the name, and what I wish to know, privately, on a long slip of white newspaper; then fold it over some twenty times. It is sealed with mucilage. He lays it on the table, and his hand writes the communication. He knows nothing of what I have written.

I have thus given in detail the facts as they have occurred with me. I do not expect those who have never examined this subject to believe it; I don't know that I ought to expect it of them. I confess I could not, until several months patient investigation. I have this consolation, however: I know that there will be a time when all must believe. I can, therefore, cheerfully receive whatever may be said of me, or the book, in perfect good humor. I hope, however, none will take the extreme ground that my good friend, Brother Poston, did, and, like him, regret it when they pass to the spirit world.

If any wish to know anything further of my views of spirit intercourse, I will say that I do most sincerely believe it to be true. There are, however, some who believe it, whose minds are led off into wild notions, as Judge Edmunds says, in a letter recently published, which he gave me:

"The time seems to be approaching which I anticipated,

some eighteen years ago, would come, when Spiritualism would become so prevalent that all sorts of 'notions' would seek to avail themselves of its popularity to spread their impurities and follies broadcast among the people. My idea is to teach Spiritualism purely and by itself, and not have it connected with, or be held responsible for any of the ordinary topics of the day. Whatever might be the opinion of individual Spiritualists upon any of such topics—Republicanism or Democracy, Free Love or San Domingo, Free Trade or Protection, Monarchy or Communism, etc.—let every one enjoy his own opinion with the utmost freedom, but not mingle Spiritualism with any of them, so as to make it, in any one's view, responsible either for the good or ill there might be in them. The constant injunction of Spiritualism to us is for us to progress in purity."

If we could divest from this subject "notions" which some have who believe in it, and take the simple question of Spirit Communion, as taught in the Bible, the Church would receive it as she did in the early days of Christianity. But alas! to many, as soon as the subject of Spiritualism is mentioned, there arise in the mind all those isms which some people would like to attach to this glorious subject.

After I had given the preceding copy to the printer, for the end of the book, I called on Dr. Mansfield, June 5, for the purpose of getting some further personal communications from my relatives. I therefore asked, Will my dear Mollie speak to her dear children now?

"Bless you! bless you, Samuel! for this, another opportunity of speaking with you. You would have me talk more particularly to our dear ones. Well, Samuel, as they cannot understand how it is mother talks to them through a stranger organism, you will be so kind as to instruct them how you get these communications. Give them all the light you can, for it will give them a better idea of your forthcoming book, when they read it. Oh that the dear ones could see the truth as you do. But, Samuel, have patience, and, little by little, will they behold the light gleaming through that sectarian darkness which obscures the light of heaven, which is trying to force its way to their anxious minds. Tell them mother is with them, day by day. Tell them to seek the truth of spirit intercourse, and know in what relations they stand to the spirit world. You are doing a work, dear Samuel, that millions yet unborn will rise up, after you are a dweller of the land of souls, and call you blessed.

"Brother Parsons, who died at Louisville, Ky., says, 'Tell your husband to be firm, not to fear whatever the would-be wise may say of his doing, but follow out the promptings of that monitor within, which is the divine within him. Some in authority will, no doubt, do their best to persecute him for the step he has taken in publishing to the world his honest convictions. But they can not harm a hair of his head, so long as he does his work fearlessly.' He says the Church attempted to stop his mouth, because of liberal utterances. But he defied them to argue the matter of who was right and who was wrong.

"He says Brother Sehon, who preached his funeral sermon, did not do him justice, and for that brother he has yet to suffer. Excuse this rambling communication, Samuel, and believe me your ever faithful and loving wife,

"MOLLIE."

Will Brother Wm. K. Poston speak to his wife and children through this medium?

"God bless you, Brother Watson, for this opportunity not only of speaking with you again, but the thought that I can speak to my now lonely darlings at home. They will be slow to believe that their husband and father, who was so bitter against this spiritual theory while he lived on earth, should now write to them in this way; but if they will credit one word of this, it will be because YOU, Brother Watson, have furnished it to them.

"Tell them Spiritualism is as true as that the sun shines out at noonday. Tell them to seek it with all their strength. And I now ask, my dear wife, to write me and the dear ones, and let us respond. Tell Miller his dear ones would speak with him and his.

"WM. K. POSTON."

Will my sister Mary speak to her husband and children?

"DARLING ONE—Your sister Mary is not present this morning to speak. How delighted would she have been to have sent a few words to her lonely ones. But, Samuel, you can say to them that they are the constant watch-care of the dear wife and mother. She is with them much of the time when not on duty. Tell them they will meet her again, never more to be separated. Your own dear

"MOLLIE."

Will my old friend and Brother, Q. C. Atkinson, speak to me?

"Thank you, Brother Watson, for this notice. Had you not have thought of me I could not have wondered at it, for so extensive and so numerous are your spirit friends. I only wonder you think of them so readily. You are doing a work that will tell not only in your generation, but in succeeding generations. Would that the M. E. Church would awake to this spirit of Wesleyanism—what a light would they shed over the world with their countless numbers. Never mind, Brother, your book will be a fire that will ignite and set on fire the shocks of superstition and bigotry which are everywhere seen in the Church, South and North, and burn them out and out.

"Tell my dear ones I am with them daily. Tell them the time hastens when we shall one and all be gathered into one happy, unbroken circle, to dwell together to all eternity. Your brother, Q. C. ATKINSON."

Has my mother a word for her son before the hour is out?

"Bless you, my son; bless you. Could you see and know how much you have done toward making happy souls on this side of the river termed Death-change, you would say you had been amply refunded for all your trouble in coming to talk with them.

"Now Samuel, my son, you will yet think of more after you get away home; so, then, allow us to advise you from time to time. To your dear ones, one and all, tell them I bless them as I bless you.

"Do allow your Brother, Parsons, to say a word to you.
"Your mother, SUSANNAH WATSON."

Will Dr. Parsons speak to me?

"BROTHER WATSON—I hoped to live long enough to see the M. E. Church alive to the spirit of true Methodism.

"I, for years, saw and felt the importance of a renovation of that Church, and talked as plainly as the people would well bear it, until within three years of my departure I was forced to give vent to my long pent-up feeling, and give the world to know where I stood. Could I have lived five years longer I would have cried aloud, even from the house-top, if need be, and proclaim what I know from external knowledge to be truth and light from the world beyond.

"Say to Brother Sehon he lacked the courage to even allude to my views of spirit intercourse while speaking over my mortal remains. I had thought him more courageous. He will hear from me again.

"Go on, Brother, I will be with you; you need not fear.
"C. B. PARSONS."

Being desirous to hear once more from a few of my friends before leaving for home, I called again on Dr. M.

LAST HOUR WITH DR. MANSFIELD.

"Thank you, thank you, my dearest of earth ones. I have not been absent from you since you came North, or to New York. I have done all I could to assist you to control your thoughts, and to arrange them in book form. Truly you have done a good work, one that will redound to your present and future well-being. As to the dear ones now living, I know not what more can be said. Tell them, one and all, that I am with them as often as my duties will permit me. I will not specify any one in particular, but what I say to *one* will equally apply to all. Bless you, dear Samuel, for those loving notices. It will give me pleasure to talk with you from time to time.

"Bless you, again bless you.
          "Your angel wife,   MOLLIE."

"Thank you, dear Bro. Watson, for this another opportunity of speaking to you before you return to that city which to us was, and now is, so dear—Memphis. Tell them, one and all, that if they would be happy there—and when they come to see as I do—to seek that light which comes from above through the medium of mortal agency.

"If you call at Louisville, say to your Bro. Rivers that I had a long talk with the General, and with his sister, Fanny Gillespie, his two spirit wives, Mary Ann and Elizabeth, and Mrs. Minerva Scruggs. Tell Rivers to look aloft, and dare to proclaim what he finds welling up in his soul from day to day. C. B. Parsons says tell Bro. Rivers if he would be happy, and make the people happy, to feed them with food which comes from on high—to allow no man to declare to him how he shall speak, or what he may speak—obey the voice within, that points him to a light that will not change in heaven. Say to my family, one and all, that a husband and father is with them; to make the best and the most of the life in the body; let their motto be to do good every time.

"To my brethren at the bar, tell them to live for eternity—as they measure to others, so SHALL it be measured to them in the sphere-land.

  "Your friend and brother, WM. K. POSTON."

Will my father-in-law, Allen Dupree, speak to me?

"How can I sufficiently reward you, Samuel, for allowing me to talk with you, if but a word? I have several times attempted to control, but some one having more potent control would take the medium from me, and I had to stand back; but now, as the way is open, I would say, thank God, our heavenly Father, you was ever permitted to be an associate of my dear daughter.

"I have watched your doings, and in all your labors of love to my dear child, and to your fellow-mortals generally, your ways have pleased me; in other words, you have done just right. Say to the dear ones, one and all, that we are often with them, although they do not see us. Tell them to live, day by day, as they will wish they had when they are called home—that life in the body was given to prepare for the life beyond. Tell them we shall meet by and by, never again to be separated. Samuel, my son, rejoice, for your mission is complete.

  "Your father-in-law, ALLEN DUPREE."

(I wish to make one remark about him. Some years after I married his daughter, he told me that from the day of her birth he had made it a matter of prayer that she might marry a Methodist preacher. Few Methodists have ever offered up such prayers, I presume. He was for many years a pillar in the Church.)

Has my father anything further to say to me?

"Well, Samuel, my son, I am always pleased to talk with you; yes, above all of those my dear ones, for in your course of life you have ever had for your motto equal rights and justice between man and man; and have ever sustained yourself in those protestations to the world. But the crowning act of your life is the legacy you leave to your fellow-men in the publication of your experiences and your object of living as you have. Blessed, blessed is the reward awaiting you. Your dear mother, Susannah, joins me in love to you.

"Your father,   LEVIN WATSON."

"Is there any one else who wishes to speak to me?" I asked; when was written:

"BRO. WATSON—Although we never personally met on earth, yet I have kept track of you for years. Now and then I caught sight of your truthful sheet, and was ever pleased with the spirit in which you conducted it. You have, by your independent action, erected to your memory a monument that time will never efface. I thank you for the willingness on your part to give my sayings a place in your book. Had I have met with you earlier, I would have said more.

"But you have a complete book as it is. I opine for you not only a ready sale, but a large one, indeed.

"God bless you, Brother,   C. B. PARSONS."
"June 7, '72."

I have thus given a truthful history of my visits to Dr. Mansfield, and all the communications received through him, with the exception of two, for others, in which I have no concern. I am aware that most persons who will read this, do not understand how it is done, nor can I tell them, so as to make them comprehend it perfectly. I wrote the name and what I wanted privately, rolled it up securely, in sometimes fifteen or twenty folds of paper, and laid it on the table. After a few moments he would write, not only with reference to what I asked, but frequently referring to things not thought of or known by me.

My interviews have been seven, embracing just eight

hours in the aggregate. I have had but little conversation with him, as his time is demanded by others.

There was no one waiting to-day, and, as it was my last interview, I asked him some questions. He says he sees the person who is communicating, but rarely ever mentions it, as many would become excited, so as to unfit them for their interview. He says he has been seeing spirits all his life, as far back as he can remember.

I have now completed my task, and glad I am of it. I have done just what I felt I must do, or suffer mentally here, if not hereafter. I know I have been honest in all I have done, and am willing to meet the Judge of all the earth. I do not, therefore, fear what man may do or say. I do know that, whatever they may think of these things here, that very soon after they pass over the river they will know the truth of them. I leave the book and the reader in the hands of my heavenly Father, praying his blessings upon them.

Having a little space on the last page, I clip from the last issue of the *Western Methodist* the concluding paragraph of an obituary notice written by a Presiding Elder of my conference, who is a nephew of ex-Governor Harris; also, two verses, from the same paper, peculiarly applicable to the stand taken by myself on the subject of ministering spirits:

"Some days before his death he said, 'My stay on earth is short; but all is right. I have not a cloud, not a shadow, not a doubt. Five minutes before he breathed his last, he turned his face to the wall, and spoke familiarly to his mother, who had been in heaven thirty-five years; then calmly passed away from earth's sorrows to heaven's joys. I write no eulogium upon the dead. His life of consistent piety is a monument more lasting than brass.
"W. T. HARRIS."

"There is no death. An angel form
 Walks o'er the earth with silent tread,
And bears our best loved things away,
 And then we call them 'dead!'

"And ever near us, though unseen,
 The dear, immortal spirits tread;
For all the boundless universe
 Is life—there is no death!"

www.ingramcontent.com/pod-product-compliance
Lightning Source LLC
Chambersburg PA
CBHW020905230426
43666CB00008B/1316